FAMILY OF FAITH
LIBRARY

W9-BJR-835

Writing About Curious Things

Amsco books by Joan D. Berbrich

Fifteen Steps to Better Writing
Laugh Your Way Through Grammar
Macbeth: A Resource Book
101 Ways to Learn Vocabulary
Reading Around the World
Reading Today
Thirteen Steps to Better Writing
Wide World of Words
Writing About Amusing Things
Writing About Curious Things
Writing About Fascinating Things
Writing About People
Writing Creatively
Writing Logically
Writing Practically

Family of Faith Library

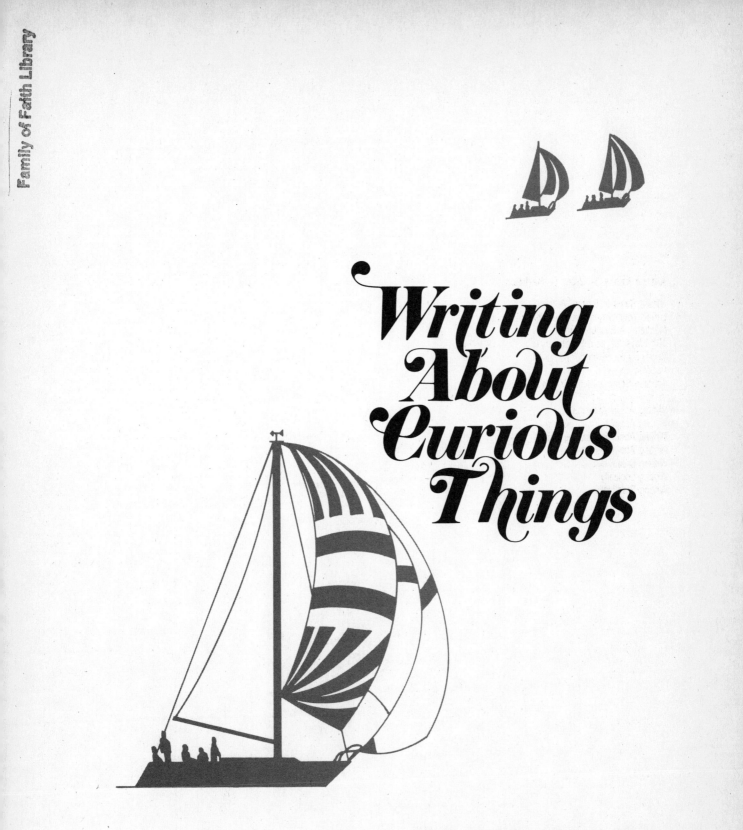

Writing About Curious Things

Joan D. Berbrich, Ph.D.

Dedicated to serving

AMSCO

our nation's youth

When ordering this book, please specify:
either **R 233 W** or WRITING ABOUT CURIOUS THINGS.

AMSCO SCHOOL PUBLICATIONS, INC.
315 Hudson Street   New York, N.Y. 10013

ISBN 0-87720-394-6

Copyright © 1981 by AMSCO SCHOOL PUBLICATIONS, INC. No part of this book may be reproduced in any form without written permission from the publisher.

Printed in the United States of America

TO THE STUDENT

People are curious. When you were a three-year-old, you drove your parents crazy with questions like these:

> "Why is the sky blue?"
> "Why can't I fly if I try real hard?"
> "What makes cement so hard?"
> "Where does the moon go when the sun comes out?"

You probably don't ask questions like these any more—and that's a shame!

Be CURIOUS.

Be CURIOUS about the world around you. Why is a barber's pole painted with alternating stripes of red and white? Which is the most popular comic strip? How far can you travel on motorized roller skates on a pint of gas? What do giraffes' tails, elephants' hairs, and six-foot stones have in common?

Be CURIOUS about your daily life. How long a line can you draw with one pencil? Why are denims called *denims?* Who ever dreamed up bread? How come your dog can hear better than you can?

Be CURIOUS about yourself. How long would your hair be if you didn't cut it *ever?* Why do you like to spend time in shopping malls? Why does your mother get angry when you leave the cap off the tube of toothpaste? Why is a bathtub shaped like a bathtub? Wouldn't it be more fun if it were shaped like a boot, or a sofa, or a bag?

Be CURIOUS about everything: about cookies and telephones and pigs; about money and bumper stickers and weather; about robots and fast-food restaurants and tin cans. Be CURIOUS about the sun: about how it affects our lives. Be CURIOUS about the fifty states that make up this nation of ours.

"All right," you say. "I'm CURIOUS. Now what? How do I find the answers?"

You can do what you did when you were three: ask questions. And *sometimes* you will get good answers.

But there's a better way: *find the answers yourself*.

> You can conduct polls and draw your own conclusions.
> You can take notes on people and their activities.
> You can check an encyclopedia or a dictionary, or the *Guinness Book of World Records* or Kane's *Famous First Facts*.
> You can keep your eyes open, noticing bumper stickers and weather signs and people's habits.
> You can even make a list. (You'll be surprised to discover how much you can learn about all sorts of things just by making lists!)

"But what," you ask, "does all this have to do with writing?"

It has everything to do with it. Writers write to share curious information with others. But more often they write because they themselves are curious.

They are curious about animals. How does a pet affect its owner? (Steinbeck found out in *The Red Pony*. Marjorie Rawlings found out in *The Yearling*.)

They are curious about the love of money or gold. (Stevenson used this as the basis of *Treasure Island*.)

They are curious about war. (See *Hiroshima* by John Hersey or *April Morning* by Howard Fast.)

They are curious about cars (*Hot Rod* by Henry Felsen); about rivers (*Huckleberry Finn* by Mark Twain); about fishing (*The Old Man and the Sea* by Ernest Hemingway); about space travel (*Space Cadet* by Robert Heinlein); about the strange inhabitants of other planets (*The War of the Worlds* by H. G. Wells).

Because they are curious, they . . . first, find out all they can about a particular subject; and second, write about it.

As they write, they find new ideas popping up; they find they have strong opinions, where before, they had no opinions at all; they *learn!*

Try it. Jot down in your notebook all you know about—PICKLES. What do they taste like? What kinds of pickles are there? What do they look like? Who likes them and who doesn't? What do you like to eat them with? When do you like to eat pickles? Do they come in jars or cans or barrels or what? Do you eat them occasionally or regularly? Would you like one for breakfast? Why, or why not?

Go to the library. Find out the history of the pickle. How is a pickle made? How many are sold a year? Where did the word "pickle" come from? How long have pickles been around? Are there any famous quotations about pickles?

Go to a supermarket. Study the shelves that house pickles. How many kinds of pickles are there? What are their names? How do they look?

Take a poll. Ask six people: "Do you like pickles? Why, or why not? When do you eat them? Why?"

By now you know a great deal more about pickles than you did before. Examine your own mind. Do you have an idea about pickles that is new and interesting? Have you learned anything about human nature? Is there an anecdote or a fact or a theory you would like to share?

If you can answer "yes" to any of the above questions, then you're ready to write—because you truly have something to say. And that, after all, is the key to writing well: to have something to say.

You see? You can write well—*if* you are CURIOUS! So look it up; check it out; investigate. Satisfy your curiosity. Good luck (I'm curious: *why* do we say that?) and good writing!

Joan D. Berbrich

TO THE TEACHER

"The overcurious are not overwise," said the playwright Massinger. Pope believed that anyone too curious "will often be stung for his curiosity." And Byron, in *Don Juan*, declared: "I loathe that low vice curiosity."

All this may have been true in the past, but in our own time, the besetting sin is *lack* of curiosity.

We live in an age of wonders, and yet we have lost wonder.

We live in an age of curious things, and yet we have lost curiosity.

We accept, without question, that images waft through the air and appear as if by magic on our television screens. We grow bored at pictures of the moon and of the planets photographed by our unmanned spacecraft. We hear of a heart transplant and nod dully and wonder if it is covered by hospitalization.

As for little things—we accept these even more unquestioningly. Pencils? Roller skates? The sun? Hmmm. We never ask ourselves where they came from, what magic they have wrought in human society.

We have become passive spectators at the game of life; yet only participants can appreciate the game fully.

The time has come for a rebirth of curiosity: for a resurgence of the questing spirit.

> Edmund Burke said: "The first and simplest emotion which we discover in the human mind is curiosity."
> James Stephens said: ". . . Hunger and love and curiosity are the great impelling forces of life."
> Richard Whately said: "Curiosity is as much the parent of attention as attention is of memory."

As teachers, we are concerned with the near-collapse of writing and of writing skills. Is not the dearth of good writing directly related to the dearth of curiosity? Homer wrote first to understand and then to share his curiosity about his age. So did Virgil. So did Milton, and Shakespeare, and Shaw, and O'Neill.

If we are to teach students to write clearly and well, then we must follow the example of the masters. We must whet their curiosities, encourage them to find the answers, and help them to think, *through writing*.

That is exactly what this book is designed to do. The first page of each chapter gives bits of information—the type to make one gasp with surprise, to make one (we hope) begin to ask questions. The second page suggests vocabulary appropriate to the subject— to make thinking and writing possible. The second page also urges students to find more information, to probe, and explore, and conclude. The third and fourth pages teach the specific skills needed to organize one's thoughts and to express them. The fifth and sixth pages lead the student to joint thinking-and-writing, to an expression of the curious, to understanding, and to the drawing of conclusions.

Curiosity—motivation, really—is of primary importance; and a relevant vocabulary and research almost equally so. But other skills are also necessary to the young writer.

Techniques are important: the use of various types of sentences, the use of various lengths of sentences; the use of parallel structure, of revision, of graphic illustration; the use of paraphrase, of prepositional phrases, of action verbs. So these, too, have their place in this text.

Other techniques, often considered esoteric for the young, are important: alliteration and onomatopoeia, similes and puns. These are not the flesh of writing; but they are the attire, the ornament. So these, too, have their place.

Repetition is vitally important, for little learning occurs without it. For this reason, parallel structure, for example, is introduced in Chapter 6, appears again in Chapter 8, and then again in Chapters 20, 21, and 25. Descriptive writing is taught in Chapters 1, 3, 14, 17, 18, 20, 23, and 25. This repetition, over a year's work, should result in permanent learning and frequent application.

It is difficult—and probably unnecessary—to expect young students to spend too much time on one type of writing. So this text is designed to move the students easily and frequently among all the types. During the year they will try their hand at the couplet and the quatrain, the limerick and the slogan, the anecdote and the fable. They will work on formal and informal essays, on letters and notes, on writing that is descriptive, persuasive, expository, and autobiographical.

All the above are important, yet the most important surely is that divine curiosity that separates humans from all other living creatures. Only we can wonder and ask; only we can understand and answer. More than two centuries ago, Samuel Johnson said: "Curiosity is one of the permanent and certain characteristics of a vigorous intellect." Let us give this great gift to our students . . . one that will help them to write more effectively and to live richer lives.

Joan D. Berbrich

CONTENTS

Writing About Curious Things

1. ALL HAIL TO HAIR!

The wolf said: "Little pig, little pig, let me come in!"
And the pig replied: "No, no, by the hair of my chinny, chin, chin!"

That little pig was smart. For if there's anything that everybody knows about and is fascinated by, it's HAIR! Since human beings first walked on this earth, they have admired hair and sometimes worshipped it. They make straight hair curly, and curly hair straight. They let it grow, and they cut it. They twist it into strange shapes, they shave it off, and they add false hair: wigs. And all this has been going on for centuries. Consider...

1 . . . The longest hair recorded belonged to a monk in India, Swami Pandarasannadhi. In 1949, his hair measured 26 feet.

2 . . . Students in Harvard in 1655 were forbidden to wear long hair.

3 . . . In the Bible, when Delilah cut off Samson's seven locks, he lost his strength and was captured by the Philistines. When his hair grew back, he tore down the supporting pillars of the house and destroyed his enemies.

4 . . . Hans Steininger was a chief magistrate in Austria. His beard was 8 feet, 9 inches long. When he went for a walk, he wrapped it around his neck. On September 28, 1567, it slipped, he tripped over it, fell down stairs, and was killed.

5 . . . In ancient Rome, beards went in and out of fashion. The Emperor Hadrian had an ugly scar and a big wart on his chin, so he grew a beard. Everyone else then did, too. But the Emperor Commodus had nothing to do and enjoyed shaving. So off came the beards!

6 . . . In modern times, hair styles go in and out of fashion, too. Brigitte Bardot made the tousled look popular. Mia Farrow popularized the urchin cut. And the Beatles with their long hair started a long-lasting style for males.

7 . . . Hair grows faster in warm weather. Changes in moisture will cause a hair to lengthen or shorten by one-third.

8 . . . Julius Caesar became bald quite early. He hated it. He urged the Roman Senate to grant him the right to wear a laurel-wreath crown. They did—and this may have been the first royal crown!

ANTONYMS

Antonyms **are words that have opposite meanings.** FINE hair is the opposite of COARSE hair—so FINE and COARSE are antonyms. Can you find antonyms for the following adjectives?

CURLY hair is the opposite of _____ hair.

LONG hair is the opposite of _____ hair.

THICK hair is the opposite of _____ hair.

DARK hair is the opposite of _____ hair.

BUSHY hair is the opposite of _____ hair.

A HAIR VOCABULARY

To describe hair intelligently, you will want to be familiar with certain words.

beard—the hair on the chin and cheeks of a man

mustache (or **moustache**)—shaped hair on a man's upper lip

whiskers—the unshaven hair on a man's face, either beard or mustache

sideburns—the hair growing down the sides of a man's face in front of the ears

peruke or **wig**—a covering of artificial or human hair worn on the head

toupee—a small wig worn to cover a bald spot

queue—a long braid of hair that hangs down the back; a pigtail

pony tail—hair drawn back and fastened, so that it hangs down like a pony's tail

bob—a short haircut on a woman or child

Afro—dense frizzy hair worn naturally

crew cut—close cropped haircut for a man

Select any two of the above words or phrases. Use each of the two in a sentence.

Word #1: _____

Sentence: _____

Word #2: _____

Sentence: _____

CURIOUS ABOUT HAIR?

Start your own collection of curiosities by tracking down answers to the following questions. After each question is the name of a book that will help you. Write the answers in *complete* sentences.

1. What was the longest beard ever recorded? To whom did it belong?
   (See the *Guinness Book of World Records*.)

   _____

2. What was the longest mustache ever recorded? To whom did it belong?
   (See the *Guinness Book of World Records*.)

   _____

3. Why are *sideburns* called *sideburns?* In other words, what is the origin of the word?
   (See an unabridged dictionary.)

   _____

4. Why is a barber's pole painted with alternating stripes of red and white?
   (See Brewer's *A Dictionary of Phrase and Fable*.)

   _____

CURL A PHRASE

Below are words and phrases using the word "hair." On the facing page, write a good sentence using each word or phrase. The first phrase is completed on the next page. Write one of your own, too.

1. **"to let one's hair down"**—to say what is on one's mind; to tell what is usually kept secret

2. **"to win by a hair"**—to win by the narrowest possible amount

3. **"hair-raising"**—terrifying, horrifying

4. **"to get in one's hair"**—to annoy someone

5. **"without turning a hair"**—without showing discomfort or embarrassment

CUT A COUPLET

We started this chapter with a wolf's statement and a pig's reply. Put the two sentences together and you have a couplet.

> "Little pig, little pig, let me come in!"
> "No, no, by the hair of my chinny, chin, chin!"

A *couplet* is simply two lines that rhyme. From page 2, choose one story or fact about hair and turn it into a couplet. Like this:

> Caesar's bald head got him down
> So he invented the first royal crown!   Your turn ⟶

STYLE A SENTENCE

Just as hair styles vary for different people and different occasions, so sentence styles vary, too. Today we'll look at two sentence styles:

> the sentence that states something, and
> the sentence that asks something.

"Blondes have more fun." This is a *statement* and is called a DECLARATIVE sentence.

"Do blondes have more fun?" This is a *question* and is called an INTERROGATIVE sentence.

Notice that the declarative sentence is followed by a period, while the interrogative sentence is followed by a question mark.

Practice some sentence-styling by changing the following declarative sentences on page 2 to interrogative sentences (on the facing page).

1. Item 7, first sentence.
2. Item 8, first sentence.
3. Item 2.
4. Item 6, last sentence.
5. Item 5, second sentence. (This is a difficult one!)

CURL A PHRASE

1. OURS: When he told me the truth about last night's basketball game, *he really let his hair down!*

   YOURS: _____

   _____

2. _____

   _____

3. _____

   _____

4. _____

   _____

5. _____

   _____

CUT A COUPLET

_____

_____

STYLE A SENTENCE

1. _____

   _____

2. _____

   _____

3. _____

   _____

4. _____

   _____

5. _____

   _____

DESCRIBING SOMEONE'S HAIR STYLE

There are almost as many hair styles as there are people! Look around you. Select the hair style of someone you know or of someone you have seen in movies or on television. *See* in your mind's eye the face and hair of this person. Then describe it.

We will develop a paragraph on this page; you work on the facing page.

Begin with a question.

Why is my cousin so fond of hair?

Describe this person's hair.

His curly black locks mantle his shoulders, his mustache is big and bushy, and his beard extends from ear to ear!

Give more details about this person's hair or about treatment of the hair.

He spends a great deal of time washing and drying and combing and shaping it.

End with a series of short interrogative sentences.

Is he hiding behind it? Does it protect him from the cold? Does he *really* consider it attractive?

Your turn now ⟶

WRITING A FABLE

A *fable* is a very short story that teaches a lesson. Below is a fable based on item 5, page 2. Read it.

Once upon a time in ancient Rome, people were like sheep. They followed their leader wherever he led. One day the Emperor Hadrian was looking in a mirror. He *hated* the ugly scar and the big wart on his chin! But what could he do? He decided to grow a beard. Pretty soon everyone at the court imitated him and grew a beard, too. Even the commoners grew beards. Most of them didn't have any scars or warts to hide, but beards had become fashionable. So they sweltered in summer, had trouble eating soup, and wasted time every day playing with their beards.

Moral: If you imitate others, you're just making trouble for yourself.

Now *you* try writing a fable. Use any item on page 2. Especially useful are items 3, 4, 6, and 8. Use simple declarative sentences, one or two interrogative sentences, and end with a MORAL: a lesson. Have fun, too, as you explore the curious ways of humans and their HAIR!

Your turn now ⟶

DESCRIBING SOMEONE'S HAIR STYLE

_____
_____
_____
_____
_____
_____
_____
_____
_____
_____
_____

WRITING A FABLE

_____
_____
_____
_____
_____
_____
_____
_____
_____
_____
_____
_____
_____
_____
_____
_____

2. PHONE CORD FEVER

It is hard to believe that 100 years ago most people didn't have telephones! In fact, even *50* years ago, most people didn't have phones! How did they live?

How did they call a doctor? Order food? Check on a wandering son? Find a plumber? Report a fire? Talk with a neighbor? Chat, *for hours*, with a friend?

It's true, though. Alexander Graham Bell invented the telephone in 1876, but few people had a phone until much, much later. And yet today we become hysterical if a phone is out of order for a few hours. Curious, isn't it?

1 ... Teen-age boys were the first telephone operators, but they were too noisy and quarrelsome. Women quickly replaced them. The first woman operator was Miss Emma Nutt in Boston, September 1, 1878.

2 ... On January 25, 1915, Dr. Alexander Bell and his assistant, Dr. Thomas Watson, were the first two people to have a transcontinental conversation, taking place between New York and San Francisco.

3 ... The average person in the United States spends one full year of his or her lifetime on the phone ... and that means 24 hours each day of that year.

4 ... Each year about 93 million people use the Yellow Pages.

5 ... Between 1876 and 1893, the Bell Telephone Company was sued 600 times for patent infringement. It won all 600 lawsuits.

6 ... Five long-distance calls are made *every second.*

7 ... Alexander Graham Bell filed an application for a patent for the first telephone on the morning of February 14, 1876. Just a few hours later, Elisha Gray filed a similar patent. (And some people say: "Wait until tomorrow!")

8 ... The first words spoken over the telephone were by Alexander Bell to Thomas Watson: "Mr. Watson, come here. I want you!" The two men were on different floors of the same building when Bell (according to one legend) spilled acid from a battery on his trousers.

9 ... By 1974 the telephone company was using enough cable and wire to make a round trip between the earth and the sun three times.

FROM ONE, MANY

It takes up to 10,000 phones to make a telephone exchange. You can't make 10,000 words from the word TELEPHONE, but you can make quite a few. You can take the T, one E, and the N and make the word "ten"; or you can take the H, the O, the T, one E, and the L to make "hotel." Can you find at least *thirty* more words in the word TELEPHONE? (You may use each letter only as often as it is used in TELEPHONE.)

_____	_____	_____	_____	_____
_____	_____	_____	_____	_____
_____	_____	_____	_____	_____
_____	_____	_____	_____	_____
_____	_____	_____	_____	_____
_____	_____	_____	_____	

A TELEPHONE VOCABULARY

Here are a few words you should know about that marvelous invention: the TELEPHONE.

patent—a grant made to an inventor by the Government promising her or him the exclusive right to make, use, and sell the invention for a certain length of time

infringement—a violation of a law or regulation (See item 5, page 8.)

statistics—numerical data.(For example, item 5, page 8, is a statistic.)

installation—the act of putting something in place and adjusting it for service (A phone is installed; a TV set is installed.)

exchange—You're familiar with the verb *exchange*, which means to trade one thing for another. In telephone lingo, it refers to as many as 10,000 phones all having the same first three digits as their telephone numbers.

digits—are numbers. The basic telephone number has 7 digits plus an area code made up of 3 more digits. (Digits also refer to fingers and toes—the earliest way to count from one to ten!)

directory—a list of names, addresses, and other facts—especially telephone numbers

Select any two of the above words. Use each in a sentence about telephones.

Word #1: _____

Sentence: _____

Word #2: _____

Sentence: _____

CURIOUS ABOUT TELEPHONES?

Keep your collection of curiosities growing by finding answers to the following questions. Write the answers in complete sentences.

1. What was the longest telephone call ever made?
   (See the *Guinness Book of World Records*.)

   _____

   _____

2. Where was the first telephone directory issued, and how many names did it include?
   (See Kane's *Famous First Facts and Records*.)

   _____

   _____

3. Which city in the world has the largest number of telephones?
   (See any good almanac.)

   _____

INVENT A WORD

Today with new things being invented all the time, new words have to be invented to name them. An easy way to invent new words is to add a **prefix**, or syllable, to the beginning of another word.

Here's how it works. Take the word "phone" which means voice or sound. Add the prefix "tele" which means far-off, distant. Put them together and you have "telephone"— far-off voice. Isn't that a good description of the telephone: something that makes far-off voices possible?

Here are three more "tele" words: TELEVISION, TELEGRAPH, TELETHON. On the facing page, define each of the three, emphasizing the meaning of the prefix "tele." Consult a dictionary if you need help.

In your definitions, follow this format:

> "Tele" is a prefix meaning far-off, or distant, or long.
> "Phone" means voice or sound.
> "Telephone" is an instrument that makes possible distant voices.

CUT A COUPLET

You have already written a couplet (two lines that rhyme) about HAIR. Now sharpen your couplet-writing skill by writing another couplet—this time about the TELEPHONE.

For example: Whenever I feel all alone,
                        I just address my friend—the PHONE!

Your turn ⟶

STYLE A SENTENCE

You have experimented with two kinds of sentence styles: the declarative and the interrogative. Below are eight sentences. The first four are interrogative sentences: questions. On the facing page, *you* provide declarative sentences: the answers. The second four are answers. *You* provide the questions. The first sentence in each group has been completed on the next page and will serve as a guide. (All information you may need is on page 8.)

1. When did Alexander Graham Bell file an application for a patent for the first telephone?
2. Why did women replace teen-age boys as telephone operators?
3. How many long-distance calls are made every second?
4. Who were the first two people to have a transcontinental conversation?

5. The first words spoken over the telephone were by Alexander Bell to Thomas Watson: "Mr. Watson, come here. I want you!"
6. The Bell Telephone Co. was sued 600 times for patent infringement between 1876 and 1893.
7. About 93 million people use the Yellow Pages each year.
8. By 1974 the telephone company was using enough cable and wire to make a round trip between the earth and the sun three times.

INVENT A WORD

television: _____

_____

_____

telegraph: _____

_____

_____

telethon: _____

_____

_____

CUT A COUPLET

_____

_____

STYLE A SENTENCE

1. Alexander Graham Bell filed an application for a patent for the first telephone on the morning of February 14, 1876.

2. _____

_____

3. _____

_____

4. _____

_____

5. What were the first words spoken over the telephone?

6. _____

_____

7. _____

_____

8. _____

_____

TAKE A POLL

Have you ever wondered what your world would be like if telephones suddenly ceased to exist? The New York Telephone Company did, and it took a poll of its subscribers. Here are some of the answers they received when they asked their subscribers what they would miss most without telephone service.*

> *Telling my husband "I love you" while he's at work.*
>
> H.U., Brooklyn

> *I wouldn't be able to call my grandparents. I would always have to go all the way to Connecticut.*
>
> S.G., 9, Huntington

> *The security of knowing that any kind of help I might require is only a telephone call away!*
>
> C.M., Binghamton

Take your own poll. Ask five people (not all the same age) what they would miss most without telephone service. Write their answers on the facing page.

USE A POLL

Finally, select from your five answers the idea that interests you most.

OURS: that the telephone aids the cause of romance   YOURS ———→

Now write a paragraph about this idea, similar to the one below. Begin with a *generalization:* a sentence that states your idea briefly.

Start with a generalization.	When Alexander Graham Bell invented the telephone in 1876, he probably didn't realize that he was playing Cupid.
Add three examples to support your generalization.	Boys call girls and girls call boys to make dates and to chat for hours. Brides call bridesmaids about gowns and rehearsals, and grooms call stores about tuxedos. Wives call husbands to say, "I love you!"
End with a question that relates to your generalization.	Can you imagine what would happen to love and romance if the telephone didn't exist?

Notice that one of the three examples comes straight from the poll. It's your turn now. Start writing!

___

*Quotations reprinted with permission from the article, "Readers say: telephones are here to stay," published in HELLO, a newsletter printed monthly by the New York Telephone Company.

TAKE A POLL

1. _____
   _____
2. _____
   _____
3. _____
   _____
4. _____
   _____
5. _____
   _____

USE A POLL

Your idea: _____

Your paragraph about this idea:

_____
_____
_____
_____
_____
_____
_____
_____
_____
_____
_____
_____
_____
_____
_____
_____
_____

3. DENIM DAYS

When Levi Strauss went to San Francisco in 1850, he carried with him a wagon-load of canvas. He would, he decided, sell canvas to the miners for tents. But the miners didn't want tents—they wanted pants: good strong, durable pants. So Strauss had a brilliant idea. He hired a tailor to turn the canvas into pants and sold out!

Strauss made two changes after that. Instead of canvas, he used denim; and he riveted the corners of the pockets so they wouldn't rip under the strain of ore samples. The result? Levi's—not very different from the jeans you wear today.

In the 19th century, denim was used for the sails of clipper ships, the tops of covered wagons, tents, and sailors' pants. After Strauss got into the act, denim was used for pants for miners and farmers. In the last ten years, denim has been used for everything: pants, jackets, skirts, ponchos, tote bags, floor cushions, even bedspreads.

For these are . . . the DENIM DAYS!

1 . . . Those blue pants so loved by people around the world are called Levi's, jeans, denims, and dungarees.

2 . . . Levi Strauss's original canvas was brown, the denim used for sails was white, and most denim today is blue . . . preferably faded. However, denim comes in all colors.

3 . . . In America, 300 million pairs of jeans are sold every year.

4 . . . In order to make denim look properly old, people sandpaper them, rub them with lime dust, bury them, soak them, and bleach them.

5 . . . In 1979 Adolfo, a designer, opened a collection of jeans for the very rich. A favorite style was a pair of blue denims embroidered with $10,000 worth of diamonds.

6 . . . Levi's are so strong they have given birth to legends. One story claims that when the coupling broke between two trains, a pair of Levi's was used to hitch them together. Another swears that Levi buttons will deflect bullets. A third insists that the belt loops on Levi's are so strong they can support workers falling from scaffoldings!

7 . . . Jeans are often worn skin-tight. Why? Because cowboys who spend hours every day in the saddle need them wrinkle-free to prevent saddle sores.

8 . . . Everyone loves jeans. An $8 pair, when smuggled into Russia, sold for $90.

PREFIX PLAY

You already know the prefix "tele," meaning far-off, as in *telephone*. Here's another prefix: "auto." AUTO means self-propelled. An *autobiography* is a biography written (or propelled) by one's *self*. Define each of the following, using *self* in each definition.

1. automobile (mobile means moving) _____

2. autograph (graph means writing) _____

3. automatic (matic means willing) _____

A DENIM VOCABULARY

texture—the way the surface of a fabric looks and feels

durable—strong; long-lasting

casual—informal; suitable for everyday use

appliqué—a decoration or trimming attached to a piece of material or clothing

rivet—a metal bolt or pin used to join two objects

deflect—to turn aside (See item 6, page 14.)

smuggle—to take something somewhere without permission (See item 8, page 14.)

Select any two of the above words. Use each of the two in a well-written sentence.

Word #1: _____

Sentence: _____

Word #2: _____

Sentence: _____

CURIOUS ABOUT DENIM?

You know why Levi's are called Levi's—because Levi Strauss was the first to make and sell them. But do you know why denims are called denims? Or why jeans are called jeans? Or why dungarees are called dungarees? You can find out—in a dictionary.

At the end of a definition, the origin of a word is usually given. Find out the origins of DENIMS, JEANS, and DUNGAREES. Then answer these questions, in complete sentences.

1. Where did the fabric, DENIM, originate? _____

_____

_____

2. Why are JEANS called JEANS? _____

_____

_____

3. What is the origin of the word DUNGAREES? _____

_____

_____

4. What do the origins of *all three* of the above words have in common? _____

_____

_____

Curious, isn't it, how new words are coined (created) and come into our language?

STYLE A SENTENCE

You know the *interrogative* sentence: "Why do you wear jeans?"
You know the *declarative* sentence: "I wear jeans because they're comfortable."

But do you know the *imperative* sentence? "Put those jeans in the wash today."
Or the *exclamatory* sentence? "Those jeans—they're gorgeous!"

An imperative sentence gives an order, a command.
An exclamatory sentence expresses strong feeling and is followed by an exclamation point. (!)

Using the information on pages 14 and 15, create examples of the four sentence styles. Write them on the facing page.

CREATE YOUR DENIM AUTOBIOGRAPHY

Some years ago Levi Strauss and Company sponsored a contest for the best decorated denims. They received 10,000 entries and exhibited the 75 best all over this country and Europe. Later four men took 145 of the entries and turned them into a book.*

Entrants (people who entered the contest) tried dozens of different techniques. They sewed or glued on appliqués; they embroidered; they added braid; they decorated with special paints. They quilted, stenciled, and attached rhinestones or nailheads. They also used dozens of themes. One pair of denims represented California with the missionaries on one leg, the miners on the other, and modern California on the back.

Judy Manley, an entrant from Honolulu, Hawaii, decorated her denim jacket with bits of clothing from her family and friends, with high school pins and a long-broken wristwatch. Later she said: ". . . my jacket is for me a remembering of roots, a chronicle of what has been and who I am . . . I wear the jacket the way one carries the things of yesterday into the now."

Your assignment is to design a pair of denims that will carry "the things of yesterday into the now"—for *you*. On the facing page is the outline of a pair of pants. Draw and write *your* autobiography on them. You can include references to where you live, to your past, and to your present. You can include likes and interests. Below, one leg of a pair of denims has been designed to help you get started . . . but you design both legs and the back. (Before you begin, read page 18. It may help you organize your ideas.)

Included on the one leg are—

1. A large red apple (New York City)
2. A horse's head (favorite interest)
3. An ice-cream cone (favorite food)
4. A book (favorite pastime)
5. A heart encircling the name Bob (a close friend)

---

*AMERICAN DENIM, by Richard M. Owens, Tony Lane, Peter Beagle, and Baron Wolman. Published by Harry N. Abrams, Inc. N.Y. 1975.

STYLE A SENTENCE

Interrogative Sentence: _____

_____

Declarative Sentence: _____

_____

Imperative Sentence: _____

_____

Exclamatory Sentence: _____

_____

CREATE YOUR DENIM AUTOBIOGRAPHY

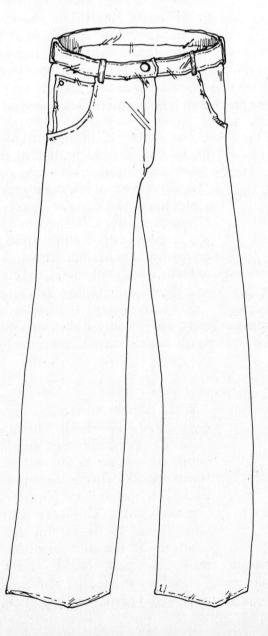

WRITE YOUR DENIM AUTOBIOGRAPHY

If someone else writes the story of your life, that's a *biography*. If *you* write the story of your own life, that's an *autobiography*. Your illustrated denims are a kind of outline of *your* autobiography. They "list" all the things you consider important in your life. First read the sample autobiography below; then write your brief autobiography, using your illustrated denim outline as a guide. (As you write, you may wish to change the order of the items. Feel free to do so.)

I. Write your first paragraph about one leg of your denims. Start with a generalization. Then describe briefly each item. Here is a sample paragraph.

Start with a generalization.	One leg of my denims illustrates my likes. It starts with a big, bright red apple. This is New York City where I live. Next comes a horse's head. I first fell in love with horses in the park, and I hope someday to be a veterinarian. The third item is an ice-cream cone, my favorite food! The fourth is a book. Without books, I wouldn't know about horses, or denims, or anything. And the final item, just below the pocket, is a heart for "Bob"—my best friend!
List items and give brief reasons as to why they are included.	
Use one exclamatory sentence, if possible.	

II. Write your second paragraph about the other leg of your denims.

Again—start with a generalization.	The other leg of my denims is a picture map of places I've visited. Starting at the bottom is a farmhouse and corral. That's my grandmother's farm in Maine. Above that is Disneyland. We went there when I was ten, and I'll never forget it. That third item, a tiny grocery store, belongs to Mr. Thomasini, one of my favorite people. I stop and visit almost every day on my way home from school. He has the best pickles in the world! Northeast of the store is the skating rink, and those little figures are supposed to be skaters. Can you recognize Bob? The last item is a subway train, not because I like them but because I spend so much time in them. Notice the graffiti!
List items and explain why each is included.	
Use an exclamatory sentence or an interrogative sentence to break up your paragraph.	

III. Write your third paragraph about the back of your denims.

Follow the same procedure as above.	When they're worn out, I may cut the legs off my denims and make shorts. That way I'll lose most of my favorite things and places. But I'll never lose the most important—those on the seat of my pants! The first figure on the left is a horse running—with *me* on his back. That tuft of hair tied to the belt loop is from my first pony, Star. The large hoof print in the middle reminds me to be careful around horses—and reminds me of the only time Star kicked me! I'd been teasing him and deserved the kick. On the far right I've embroidered spurs, reins, and a saddle. As you can see, I love horses—and my jeans show it!
Vary your sentence styles.	
Be a bit humorous.	
End with a brief sentence that sums up your denim autobiography.	

WRITE YOUR DENIM AUTOBIOGRAPHY

I. _____

_____

_____

_____

_____

_____

_____

_____

II. _____

_____

_____

_____

_____

_____

_____

_____

III. _____

_____

_____

_____

_____

_____

_____

_____

4. IT'S A DOG'S LIFE

"Who loves me will love my dog also," said St. Bernard of Clairvaux.
"The more I see of men, the better I like my dog," said Frederick the Great.

Every child wants a puppy. Teenagers confide in their dogs. Men and women find them uncritical and comforting. Old people turn to them for protection and companionship.

What is this four-legged, tail-wagging, arrogant, humble, destructive, protective creature called—a DOG?

... There are about 40 million dogs in the U.S.—one for every five people.

... One superstition says that a dog will howl before the death of someone in the family. Another claims that dogs can see ghosts.

... Dogs bite one out of every twenty newspaper deliverers each year.

... Two dogs came over on the *Mayflower:* a spaniel and a mastiff.

... The ancient Egyptians had a dog-headed god, called Anubis, who guided the souls of the dead to the underworld.

... Dogs have excellent hearing. What a human can hear at 175 yards, a dog can hear a half mile away. Dogs can also hear silent or supersonic whistles. Small dogs hear better than large dogs.

... According to one legend, about 10,000 years ago, a lion fell in love with a squirrel. The result? The Pekinese dog.

... Dogs have fine homing instincts. One dog, left in Seattle, Washington, deserted its new home and traveled 1800 miles to its former home in Minnesota.

... Dogs do not see well, and they are colorblind. But at night, they see better than we do.

... During World War II, dogs served in the K9 (canine!) Corps of the U.S. Army. They located wounded soldiers on battlefields, carried messages, and nosed out land mines. They could detect easily the turned-up earth that indicated a mine had been buried.

BARKING DOGS

Like dogs' barks, some words sound alike, but they have different meanings—and spellings. These words are called *homophones.*

The following sentences will make sense if you insert the correct pair of homophones in the blanks. Example: A dog does not need extraordinary _____ to recognize its own _____. The answers, of course, are *sight* and *site.* You try it.

1. Jessica wrote a _____ about a dog that never wagged its _____.

2. The _____ story is that Fido, looking for an old bone, dug the _____.

3. Because he wrecked our _____ boat, our St. Bernard was put up for _____.

4. If a dog shatters a window _____, he will almost certainly feel _____.

5. A dog may _____ a bone, but not if the bone is made of _____.

DOG VOCABULARY

There are so many words relating to dogs that one can almost create a dog dictionary. Here are just a few "doggy" words.

canine—a dog or related animal (like a wolf)

kennel—a shelter for dogs; also, an establishment that breeds and takes care of dogs

license—a document that shows that legal permission has been given to do something or to own something (Every dog must have a license.)

veterinarian—a person trained to give medical treatment to animals

rabies—an infectious disease that usually causes death and is transmitted by the bite of an infected animal

domesticated—trained to live with human beings

ordinance—a municipal law (for example, a "Curb Your Dog" ordinance)

ASPCA—American Society for the Prevention of Cruelty to Animals

muzzle—a wire or leather device placed over an animal's snout to prevent biting

vivisection—the act of dissecting (cutting apart) a living animal for scientific research

Select any two of the above words. Use one in an interrogative sentence and the other in a declarative sentence.

Word #1: _____

Sentence: _____

Word #2: _____

Sentence: _____

CURIOUS ABOUT DOGS?

Keep your collection of curiosities growing by answering these questions—in complete sentences, of course.

1. What is the smallest fully grown dog ever recorded and how much did it weigh? (See the *Guinness Book of World Records*.)

_____

2. What is the largest dog ever recorded and how much did it weigh? (See the *Guinness Book of World Records*.)

_____

3. What is the oldest dog ever recorded? (See the *Guinness Book of World Records*.)

_____

4. What is the largest litter ever recorded? (See the *Guinness Book of World Records*.)

_____

DOG DAYS

DOG DAYS are the hot, humid days of summer. Here are a few more "dog" words and phrases.

dog-eared: worn and shabby

dogged: stubborn

raining cats and dogs: raining hard

hot dog: barbecue favorite

put on the dog: dress up

dog-tired: exhausted

gone to the dogs: seedy; uncared for

doggerel: humorous or bad poetry

lucky dog: fortunate person

dog's life: miserable existence

in the doghouse: in trouble; out of favor

dog tag: military identification

dogwatch: night shift

hangdog: forlorn, unhappy

dog paddle: a swimming stroke

dog-eat-dog: selfish, ruthless

dogtrot: easy, quick gait

dogfight: battle between fighter planes

Two or more of these phrases can be combined to form a really "doggy" sentence!

As she picked up her DOG-eared book, Clara realized she would be in the DOGhouse for not first finishing the dishes.

You try it, creating three doggy sentences on the facing page. ———→

DOG DIALOGUE

Here's a real challenge. Develop a four-line dialogue with your dog. (If you don't have a dog, create an imaginary one.) The hard part is that the four lines must be written as four different types of sentences. Here's an example of a conversation between Peter and his dog, Jeff.

Peter: "Roll over, Jeff."	(imperative sentence)
Jeff: "Grrr . . .?"	(interrogative sentence)
Peter: "You're tired, that's why; and you need to rest."	(declarative sentence)
Jeff: "Awf!"	(exclamatory sentence)

Notice that each speaker's dialogue starts a new line and is placed inside quotation marks. You try it, on the facing page. ———→

DOG CATECHISM

A *catechism* is any book containing questions and answers. Using the information given on pages 20 and 21, create a brief dog catechism of five questions and answers.

Example:

Question: Why do dogs howl?
Answer: According to one superstition, dogs howl to signal the coming death of someone in the family.

Your turn ———→

DOG DAYS

1. _____

   _____

2. _____

   _____

3. _____

   _____

DOG DIALOGUE

    _____   _____

    _____   _____

    _____   _____

    _____   _____

DOG CATECHISM

1. _____

   _____

   _____

   _____

2. _____

   _____

   _____

   _____

3. _____

   _____

   _____

4. _____

   _____

   _____

5. _____

   _____

   _____

   _____

ONE DOG STORY

Almost any piece of information will trigger ideas in your head. And the information plus the ideas can be developed into a brief, interesting paragraph.

> *The ancient Egyptians had a dog-headed god, called Anubis, who guided the souls of the dead to the underworld.* What a comforting idea! Dogs are fine leaders; they guide people out of forests and down mountains. Dogs are protective; they'll do battle with the devil himself! Dogs are loyal; they won't dart off after a rabbit until they've delivered you safely to your destination. It was certainly logical of the ancient Egyptians to have a DOG-headed god to guide the souls of the dead. Wouldn't it be dreadful to have to depend on a mouse or a mosquito for that last, long journey?

Simply choose one piece of information about dogs from pages 20 and 21. Use this as your first or *topic* sentence . . . as we used the sentence from item 5, page 20, to begin *our* paragraph. Then add a few ideas of your own about that piece of information. Use a variety of sentence styles. (In the paragraph above, there are four declarative sentences, one interrogative sentence, and two exclamatory sentences.)

Ready? Go! Write your paragraph on the next page.

ANOTHER DOG STORY

Because dogs are cute and intelligent and pathetic and funny and loyal, they make good subjects for ANECDOTES. **An *anecdote* is a very short story, interesting and possibly humorous, about some event.**

This time select a piece of information from pages 20 and 21 *or* a personal experience you have had with a dog and write an anecdote.

Start with a simple introductory sentence.	Peppy is a small black-and-white dog who lives next door. She considers our yard an extension of her own. Unfortunately she's a digger, and I object to yawning craters surrounding my petunias. So I decided to put up a long hinged gate to discourage her. The next morning as I had the gate ajar while painting it, Peppy appeared. She edged toward the opening. I growled; she retreated. A few minutes later when she thought I wasn't looking, she edged toward it again. Again I growled; again she retreated. This time she sat down patiently and waited. More than a little suspicious, I kept one eye cocked and continued painting. As I worked down to the far end of the gate, Peppy weighed her chances and made a last dash for the opening. Oh, I stopped her—but anyone who tries to tell me dogs aren't intelligent should meet Peppy!
Add details.	
Notice use of repetition.	
End with punch line of story or summarizing comment.	

Keep it simple. Keep it light. And try—if possible—to include a touch of repetition. Start. . . .

ONE DOG STORY

_____
_____
_____
_____
_____
_____
_____
_____
_____
_____

ANOTHER DOG STORY

_____
_____
_____
_____
_____
_____
_____
_____
_____
_____
_____
_____
_____
_____

5. MAKE A LIST!

Why make a list? Well, a list helps you to find out what's inside your mind. A list helps you to discover what is important to you and what isn't. A list helps you to *think*.

Besides, list-making is fun. Many people make shopping lists and lists of things to do. Some make lists of cars, of foods, of admired people. The lists you are going to work on in this chapter are a little different.

Start by making (on the facing page) a list of 5 things you like, 5 things you dislike, and 5 things you would like to do. For example:

5 Things I Like

To walk along the beach in autumn
To eat just-baked cookies
To go to summer camp
To ride a bike early in the morning
To visit my grandparents

5 Things I Dislike

To get up early
To clean my room
To do the dishes
To do homework
To get dressed up

5 Things I Would Like to Do

To travel around the entire country in a van
To fly in a superjet
To be a popular TV movie star
To walk on the moon
To become a millionaire

Now it's time to use these lists. Pretend they were drawn up by a stranger. What can you learn about this stranger, just from the lists? Give the person an *alias*, another name. We'll call our "stranger" Barbara.

Begin with a generalization.

Support this generalization by referring to specific items on each of the three lists.

Notice that not *all* items are used—only those that support your generalization.

End with a prediction as to the future. (This is a good time to vary your sentence style if you haven't already done so.)

Barbara is a dreamer and a free spirit. She dislikes all the things she has to do: ordinary things like getting up early and cleaning her room. She enjoys doing things alone. She likes to walk along the beach in autumn (when there's no one else there). She likes to ride a bike early in the morning (when there's no one else around). Even her long-range goals reflect her desire to be free. Three of those goals involve traveling long distances . . . even to the moon! What will happen to Barbara in the future? It's hard to say. If she works at making her dreams come true, she may accomplish great deeds. But if she just dreams—well, that would be a sad ending, wouldn't it?

5 Things I Like

_____

_____

_____

_____

_____

5 Things I Dislike

_____

_____

_____

_____

_____

5 Things I Would Like to Do

_____

_____

_____

_____

_____

Your paragraph about the "stranger" who made up your lists:

_____

_____

_____

_____

_____

_____

_____

_____

_____

_____

_____

_____

_____

_____

_____

_____

_____

HAPPINESS IS . . . .

Here are two more lists + a chance to "read" them—to interpret them.

First make a list of 5 happy people. (Use aliases or initials to protect their privacy.) Explain briefly why each is happy.

⟶

1. Edwin: Edwin is happy when he is working on photography. And he's always doing that.
2. Janet: Janet loves animals. She's happy when she's feeding or grooming them.
3. David: David just likes people. He talks even to strangers, and he smiles a lot.
4. Maria: Maria's the busiest person I know. She's always doing something, and she seems to enjoy everything she does.
5. Jimmy: Jimmy loves to explore. As long as there is a garage or a barn, a field or a street to explore, he's happy.

Now make a list of 5 unhappy people. (It's even more important to use aliases or initials here.) Explain why each is unhappy.

⟶

1. Diana: Diana is usually miserable. She worries about her hair and her clothing.
2. Frank: Frank hates to work, and since he *has* to, he's frequently grouchy.
3. Olive: Olive isn't interested in many things. She's usually bored.
4. Kenny: Kenny gets angry when he doesn't get his way . . . so he's often unhappy.
5. Julie: Julie is always afraid someone will take advantage of her. She doesn't trust anyone.

Finished? Good. Now study both lists carefully. Think. In your opinion, what *one* factor causes happiness or unhappiness? Use this as your generalization, and support the generalization by referring to specific people on your two lists.

⟶

Generalization.

Happiness is caring; unhappiness is not caring. People are happy when they care about other people, about animals, or about their work. Edwin loves fooling around with photography. Janet loves being with animals. Jimmy loves to explore. All of them are happy—because they *care*. Olive, who is bored, obviously doesn't care about anybody or anything. Kenny has a chip on his shoulder. How can he be happy? And Julie is so afraid of trusting anyone that she lives in a lonely world. All three are unhappy— because they do not *care* for anyone or anything outside themselves. Unhappiness is letting yourself be isolated by fears. Happiness is getting involved—doing things—trusting people—*caring!*

Supporting details from lists above.

Conclusion—repeating and extending the opening generalization.

Now it's your turn. When you have finished writing your paragraph of evaluation, you should understand better than you did why some people are happy and why some are not. That's a useful thing to know. Who doesn't want to be happy? And remember— you learned this by making out a couple of lists!

HAPPINESS IS . . . .

5 happy people and why they are happy:

_____
_____
_____
_____
_____

5 unhappy people and why they are unhappy:

_____
_____
_____
_____
_____

Your paragraph explaining what, in your opinion, causes happiness or unhappiness:

_____
_____
_____
_____
_____
_____
_____
_____
_____
_____
_____
_____
_____
_____
_____

A SPECIAL DINNER PARTY

Your final challenge is—to invite ten guests for dinner! This dinner you are giving may be formal with many courses, or a simple barbecue. Your job is to make up a list of guests, ten people. They may be people you know or people you have only heard about. They may be people living now or people who lived thousands of years ago. After each name, explain briefly *why* you would invite this particular person.

$\longrightarrow$

Remember—you can have Abraham Lincoln for a guest, or Shakespeare, or John Travolta. You can have Joan of Arc or Tatum O'Neal or Thomas Edison. Exciting thought, isn't it?

Here is a list made up by one young teenager, Jeanne.

1. *Tennis player Bjorn Borg:* I like watching him play. He's great! Also, I think he's handsome!
2. *President James Earl Carter:* I would like to meet him and talk with him about the nation's problems during his administration.
3. *Playwright William Shakespeare:* I love the time era he lived in and feel I could learn a lot from him. Also, I would like to see what he thinks about modern times.
4. *Actor Erik Estrada:* I would enjoy his company immensely. Besides, he's really good-looking!
5. *Queen of England, Elizabeth II:* I would invite her to add a bit of elegance to my party. I would like to see if royalty would like to be among my guests and to get her views on the difference in the ways our countries are run.
6. *Explorer Christopher Columbus:* I would enjoy hearing him talk about how America has changed since he discovered it.
7. *Friend Emma McNeil:* She's one of my best friends, and I'd like to share the party with her.
8. *Poet Edgar Allan Poe:* I would enjoy talking to him because his poems fascinate me. I would like to find out for myself his real frame of mind.
9. *Poet Robert Frost:* I would invite him to see his reactions to the destruction that progress has caused to the once beautiful scenery he wrote about.
10. *My parents:* because they enjoy seeing the people I like (and besides, they are probably paying for the party!).

SOME THOUGHTS ABOUT MY DINNER PARTY

Now read over your list, think, and jot down a few comments about your choices.

As I look over my list, I worry that Bjorn Borg may be lonely. He'll be the only athlete there, and he may have no one to talk to. Shakespeare and Erik Estrada should have a good time. They can compare acting 400 years ago and today. Poe and Frost both wrote poems, but they were so different they may end up arguing. Elizabeth II, though, should be a help. She's had plenty of experience in making people comfortable at big parties. So has President Carter. As for my parents, Emma, and me—we'll probably sit there with our mouths open, listening, amazed at this curious collection of celebrities!

Your turn to make some thoughtful comments on the next page.

A SPECIAL DINNER PARTY

Your ten guests:

1. _____
_____

2. _____
_____

3. _____
_____

4. _____
_____

5. _____
_____

6. _____
_____

7. _____
_____

8. _____
_____

9. _____
_____

10. _____
_____

SOME THOUGHTS ABOUT MY DINNER PARTY

_____
_____
_____
_____
_____
_____
_____
_____
_____

TIME-OUT—I

When you're working hard, it always feels good to stop for a "break." After every five chapters, there will be a "Time-Out"—time to relax, to have fun! Ready?

I. More than 200 years ago, some women went in for huge and elaborate hair styles. Below is a sketch of one hair style that might well have been popular in 1777. It shows a wildly exaggerated coiffure (hairdo) that serves as the setting for Washington's Crossing of the Delaware to Trenton, 1776. Notice the soldiers rowing the boat, the flag-bearer, the confident General himself—and even chunks of snow and ice floating in the river!

Now that you have enjoyed this humorous sketch, create an equally mad coiffure for someone today. Select an event that you think deserves to be commemorated. Then, on separate paper, design a suitable hairdo and describe it.

Fun, isn't it, to let your imagination run wild? And think what a curious party you could give if you requested all guests to arrive sporting original and picturesque hairdos!

II. Now that you have created a fascinating hairdo, try coining (creating) some fascinating words! One way to coin new words is to add a prefix to another word. You know the prefixes "tele" (far-off, distant) and "auto" (self-propelled). With a little ingenuity, you can coin TELEMOBILE. What is a TELEMOBILE? Well, logically it is a moving vehicle ideal for long distances. With this in mind, we can develop a definition.

TELEMOBILE: a vehicle that can move over land and over water and that can fly; one that is ideal for traveling around the world.

Sharpen your wits by developing definitions for the following just-coined words:

AUTOVISION: _____

_____

TELEROAD: _____

_____

AUTOMEDICINE: _____

_____

Now go one step further. *You* coin three new words using the prefixes "tele" or "auto." Then define each new word.

1. _____: _____

_____

2. _____: _____

_____

3. _____: _____

_____

III. You know how important it is to have good details to support generalizations. Below are twelve assorted objects:

tin cans	ice cream	Incredible Hulk
caramel popcorn	Frankenstein	paper cups
dragons	soda bottles	Abominable Snowman
candy wrappers	cookies	candy

Next, here are three generalizations. Under each generalization, list *four* objects (from the above list) that can be used to develop it.

1. My favorite foods are all sweet.

_____   _____

_____   _____

2. Monsters are really lovable.

_____   _____

_____   _____

3. We are drowning in litter!

_____   _____

_____   _____

Words in Review

Fooling around with words can be fun. So relax—and enjoy these word games!

IV. First, take pen or pencil in hand and see if you can track down in the diagram below twenty-nine of the words used in the first five chapters. You can find them by moving from left to right, or from top to bottom. Just circle each word as you find it.

Below the diagram, as clues, are definitions. The number of blanks after each definition indicates the number of letters in the word you are looking for. Write the words on the appropriate blanks.

V	I	V	I	S	E	C	T	I	O	N	K
E	X	C	L	A	M	A	T	O	R	Y	E
T	F	A	B	L	E	M	D	O	G	R	N
E	L	T	A	U	T	O	P	U	D	I	N
R	D	E	C	L	A	R	A	T	I	V	E
I	T	C	J	O	D	A	T	L	G	E	L
N	E	H	E	S	E	L	E	I	I	T	I
A	L	I	A	S	N	I	N	N	T	C	C
R	E	S	N	W	I	G	T	E	T	O	E
I	A	M	S	A	M	O	R	I	G	I	N
A	N	E	C	D	O	T	E	E	N	N	S
N	C	O	U	P	L	E	T	A	L	L	E

1. Artificial hair worn on the head __ __ __
2. Antonym of "short" __ __ __ __
3. A two-line poem __ __ __ __ __ __ __
4. A sentence that makes a statement __ __ __ __ __ __ __ __ __ __ __
5. A very short story that teaches a lesson __ __ __ __ __
6. The lesson taught by the very short story __ __ __ __ __ __
7. A grant to an inventor promising her or him the exclusive right to make, use, and sell the invention __ __ __ __ __ __
8. A number, a toe, or a finger __ __ __ __ __
9. A prefix meaning "far-off" or "distant" __ __ __ __
10. Work pants made of denim __ __ __ __ __
11. A prefix meaning "self-propelled" __ __ __ __
12. The beginning of something; the source __ __ __ __ __ __
13. A coarse, durable fabric from which work clothes are made __ __ __ __ __ __
14. A sentence that expresses strong feeling and ends with an exclamation point __ __ __ __ __ __ __ __ __ __ __
15. A list of things to write about __ __ __ __ __ __ __
16. A metal pin or bolt used to join two objects __ __ __ __ __ __
17. A shelter for dogs __ __ __ __ __ __
18. A legal document that shows that permission has been given to do something or to own something __ __ __ __ __ __
19. A person trained to give medical treatment to animals __ __ __ __ __ __ __ __ __
20. The act of dissecting a living animal for scientific research __ __ __ __ __ __ __ __ __ __ __
21. Verb meaning to create a new word __ __ __ __ __
22. A canine; a four-legged animal __ __ __
23. A foot digit that rhymes with "doe" __ __ __
24. A short story, interesting and humorous, about some event __ __ __ __ __ __ __ __
25. A series of questions and answers __ __ __ __ __ __ __ __
26. Antonym of a "gain" __ __ __ __
27. A false name __ __ __ __ __
28. Drop a letter from "learn" to get thin! __ __ __ __
29. What you are or soon will be "a __ __ __ __ -ager"

V. ANTONYM ANTICS. Antonyms, remember, are words with opposite meanings. "Young" and "old" are antonyms. If you find the right antonyms for the eight words below, the first letters of your answers will form *another* pair of antonyms. Ready?

tall	— — — — —	near	— — —
big	— — — — — —	before	— — — — —
extraordinary	— — — — — — —	curly	— — — — — — —
domesticated	— — — —	false	— — — — —

VI. PYRAMID PLAY. Find the correct word to fit each of the following definitions, insert them on the blanks at the right, and you will construct a "D" pyramid. Can you do it in five minutes?

1. The fourth letter of the alphabet — —
2. Verb meaning "to act" — — —
3. A canine; a four-legged animal — — —
4. Verb meaning "to sketch" — — — —
5. Coarse, strong fabric often used in making jeans — — — — —
6. Toes and fingers; also numbers — — — — — —
7. Strong; long-lasting — — — — — — —
8. Conversation between two or more people — — — — — — —
9. Book listing names, addresses, and telephone numbers — — — — — — — —

VII. ALPHABET ART. There are dozens of kinds of dogs in the world. See if you can find one for each letter of the alphabet listed below. The letter "A" has been completed for you. (If you find this difficult—and you may—an encyclopedia may be helpful!)

A	**Afghan hound**	L	_____
B	_____	M	_____
C	_____	N	_____
D	_____	O	_____
E	_____	P	_____
F	_____	R	_____
G	_____	S	_____
H	_____	T	_____
I	_____	W	_____
K	_____	Y	_____

6. THE COOKIE MONSTER

Think about cookies for a minute. Think about crisp sugar cookies, and delectable chocolate chips, and no-nonsense ginger snaps. Think about saltines with cheese and graham crackers with peanut butter. Think about cookies filled with raisins and nuts and chopped dates and bits of butterscotch. Think about cream-filled sandwiches, chocolate-covered marshmallows, and cookies that leave your hands sticky with powdered sugar. Think of coin-sized cookies that you can pop into your mouth while running, and saucer-sized cookies that can serve as a lunch.

About the only characteristic that cookies share is—they are *delicious!*

1 . . . Thousands of years ago, poor people could not afford to sacrifice animals or other food to their gods. Sometimes they baked small cakes, instead, shaping them carefully to look like sheep or birds. These *may* have been the first cookies.

2 . . . Cookie dough is easily made and fairly inexpensive. With it, you can make glittering ornaments and tempting toys . . . all of which can later be eaten.

3 . . . Cookies emblazoned with the family coat of arms were once used by the nobility as calling cards.

4 . . . Frederick III, German Emperor, handed out 4,000 gingerbread likenesses of himself when he was concerned about his political future. He hoped that as the children munched tiny Fredericks, their parents would support the big Frederick.

5 . . . A well-known Chinese cookie is the fortune cookie. It is not only delicious to eat but it predicts your future, promising long life and success to most eaters.

6 . . . In colonial America, mothers and teachers baked cookie hornbooks. (A hornbook was a piece of wood covered with paper on which were inscribed the letters of the alphabet and numbers.) A good child who could identify a letter could *eat* that cookie letter.

7 . . . Years ago many weddings and christenings were commemorated with elaborately decorated cookies. Guests could keep the cookies as souvenirs (or eat them).

8 . . . Before newspapers and books were common, cookies told stories. Some depicted historical events, some portrayed important people, and some just reminded children that a schoolteacher had arrived in town and school would soon be open!

VOWEL AND CONSONANT

Which helps you to identify a word: the *vowels* (a, e, i, o, u) or the *consonants* (all the other letters)? What kind of cookie do these letters stand for? __a__e__. Can't guess? How about this way? w__f__r. You guessed *wafer*? You're right. Consonants are more important than vowels in helping us to identify words. Below are several kinds of cookies—consonants only. Complete each name by filling in the vowels.

cr__ck__r   sn__p   s__lt__n__s

b__sc__ __ts   gr__h__ms   s__ndw__ch__s

A COOKIE VOCABULARY

knead—to press, fold, stretch, etc. into a uniform mass

malleable—easy to handle; can be pressed into different shapes

palatable—pleasant tasting enough to be eaten

molds—hollow containers into which dough can be pressed to form cookies of a particular shape

commemorate—to honor the memory of; to remind people of a particular event or person

improvise—to invent something quickly; to put something together in a moment

preheat—"pre" is a prefix meaning "before"; hence, to heat before

Select any two of the above words. Use each of the two in a complete sentence.

Word #1: _____

Sentence: _____

Word #2: _____

Sentence: _____

COOKIE ADJECTIVES

Cookies are *delicious*, of course, but that doesn't tell you much about a particular cookie. Probe your memory and see if you can find *six* more specific adjectives for cookies, like the two below.

_____crunchy_____   _____   _____   _____

_____sweet_____   _____   _____   _____

CURIOUS ABOUT COOKIES?

One way to satisfy your curiosity is to ask questions.

1. Ever wonder what kind of cookie is most popular? Ask ten people: "What kind of cookie do you like best?" Write the results below in one or two sentences.

_____

_____

_____

2. Ask three adults: "Which cookie from your childhood do you remember best? Why? Is it associated with a special holiday, or occasion, or what?" Write the answers below.

_____

_____

_____

HOW TO . . .

Suppose you bake fantastic peanut-butter cookies and someone asks you for the recipe. Can you write directions that are clear and easy to follow? This is something you will be doing throughout your life: writing directions for baking cookies, or for finding a particular street, or for playing a favorite game.

You will find writing directions simple if you *begin each sentence with a verb.*

"How to Eat Saltines"

1. *Extract* six double saltines from the package.
2. *Spread* peanut butter liberally on all twelve saltines.
3. *Cut* twelve squares of yellow cheese, each about 1 inch square.
4. *Place* a square of cheese exactly in the center of each saltine.
5. *Pick* up one completed saltine and nibble at the perimeter, leaving the cheese.
6. *Move* to the center; bite into the cheese-peanut butter-saltine combination.
7. *Chew* and swallow.
8. *Proceed* to second saltine, third, etcetera, until all saltines are consumed.
9. *Wash* down with a glass of cold milk.
10. *Return* to desk to complete homework.

It's your turn now.

$\longrightarrow$

I RECOMMEND . . .

The main function (use) of a cookie is to be eaten! But as you saw on page 36, cookies have other functions as well. Cookies have been used to educate (item 6), to predict the future (item 5), to quiet the anger of the gods (item 1), and to win votes (item 4). Put your imagination to work and dream up a *new* function for cookies.

OURS: *Cookies can be used as currency (or money).*   YOURS $\longrightarrow$

Now write a paragraph supporting your recommendation. Be enthusiastic! Remember: you are trying to persuade other people to use cookies in a totally new way.

State your recommendation.

List arguments to support your recommendation.

End with a forceful or humorous comment.

I recommend that cookies be used as currency. Thanks to inflation, our money has little value. Cookies have an immediate—and obvious—value! But there are other advantages to using cookies instead of coins. You will think twice before buying if you have to turn over five delicious chocolate chip cookies for a piece of pizza. And you will think three times before swapping twenty crisp sugar cookies loaded with raisins for a single record. The very fact that you have to carry boxes of cookies with you when you go shopping will slow down the frantic purchasing trend in this country. Then, too, a cookie currency will end inflation. Everyone knows that inflation results when there is too much money in circulation. Since all of us will spend a good deal of time nibbling away at our money, inflation will soon end. Why hasn't someone thought of this simple solution before? Cookies for currency—and an end to all our problems!

HOW TO . . .

Write directions for *one* of the following:

"How to Bake _____ Cookies" (for example, Chocolate Chip)

"How to Decorate _____ Cookies" (for example, Halloween)

"How to Eat _____" (for example, a Gingerbread House)

YOUR CHOICE: _____

_____

_____

_____

_____

_____

_____

_____

_____

_____

I RECOMMEND . . .

Some suggestions to help you dream up a new function for cookies:

Cookies as code carriers for spies
Cookies as report cards
Cookies as a total diet
Cookies as building material

YOUR CHOICE: _____

_____

_____

_____

_____

_____

_____

_____

_____

_____

_____

A COOKIE STORY

Telling a story to a child is fun, as you already know if you have a younger brother or sister, niece or nephew. So create your very own children's story, based on your new function for cookies (page 38).

Our characters:	Jeremy Butler and his friend, Davy.	Yours ⟶
Our setting:	A fall day and a walk to a nearby store.	Yours ⟶
Our plot:	Jeremy and Davy set out to spend their cookie allowances but run into all sorts of problems.	Yours ⟶

As you write your story, use lots of dialogue and some repetition. Small children love repetition. And have fun. The more fun you have writing your story, the more fun some child will have listening to it! Read the story below—then write on the facing page.

"Cookies as Currency"

Jeremy Butler started out one morning in early fall. He had his week's allowance in his pockets: six sugar cookies, three chocolate chips, four graham crackers, and one large, decorated gingerbread dog.

"I think I'll buy a rocket ship," he said out loud. "Or maybe a new football."

As he walked to the store, the wind nipped his cheeks and made him hungry. "Perhaps I'll eat just two sugar cookies," he told himself. And he promptly did.

Just then a big Irish setter jumped up on him, begging. Jeremy stared at the big brown eyes and gave in. "All right," he said. "You can have the three chocolate chips." And the dog quickly gobbled them up.

A block later, Jeremy met his friend, Davy.

"I just got my allowance," Davy said. "Let's see what you got."

The two boys spread out their "allowances."

Jeremy eyed Davy's wistfully. "I *love* those chocolate-covered marshmallows," he said. "What will you swap them for?"

"I'll swap one marshmallow for your four sugar cookies," Davy said eagerly. They made the exchange, and Jeremy rapidly ate the chocolate-covered marshmallow while Davy consumed the sugar cookies.

As they continued on their way to the store, they played with Davy's Frisbee. All that running and jumping, throwing and catching really worked up their appetites; so they sat down on a bench in front of the store and decided to eat just a little more. They ate Davy's last two chocolate-covered marshmallows (one each) and divided Jeremy's delicious gingerbread dog.

Mournfully Jeremy looked at what was left of his allowance. "I have only four graham crackers now," he said sadly. "What can I buy with that?"

"Not much," said Davy. "And I have left only three saltines."

Inside the store, the boys strolled, looking at things they would like to buy. A rocket ship cost four sugar cookies and two chocolate chips. A football cost a whole gingerbread dog plus two chocolate-covered marshmallows. The only thing that cost four graham crackers and three saltines was a packet of two balloons.

"And balloons fly away," Jeremy said.

Davy nodded. "Or they break."

The two went back to the bench to think. As they thought, they nibbled away at the grahams and saltines. Suddenly Jeremy laughed. "Our problem is solved," he said. "We can't buy *anything*. We've eaten up our allowances!"

A COOKIE STORY

Your characters: _____

Your setting: _____

Your plot: _____

_____

Your story:

_____

_____

_____

_____

_____

_____

_____

_____

_____

_____

_____

_____

_____

_____

_____

_____

_____

_____

Test your story by telling it to some child. Since the subject is COOKIES, they're bound to gobble it up!

7. PENCIL POWER

"Everything begins with a pencil!" someone once said. And it's true.

You used it when you were two to draw clowns and boats and moons.

You used it when you were six to learn to write.

You use it every day—to write notes, to make lists, to record phone messages, to play tic-tac-toe.

Inventors use it, to draw designs and blueprints.

Surgeons use it, to outline the plan of an operation on a patient's body.

Scientists use it, to describe experiments performed.

Imagine what the world would be like *without* pencils!

... The very first "pencil" was probably a burnt stick used thousands of years ago by some early ancestor of ours.

... The first modern pencil came into existence by accident. In 1564 a storm uprooted a huge tree in Borrowdale, England. Where the roots had been was a large mass of almost pure graphite. Local shepherds began using it to brand their sheep.

... Pencils are usually made from cedarwood, which is soft enough to sharpen easily.

... The average pencil is sharpened 17 times during its lifetime.

... The word "pencil" comes from "pencillus"—the Latin word for little tail. The ancient Romans used a tiny brush dipped in ink. As the little brush swept across the paper, it looked for all the world like a "little tail."

... This is what it takes to produce one pencil: 40 different raw materials from 28 countries put through 125 manufacturing steps.

... According to the Pencil Makers Association, if you wanted to make your own pencil, a single one would cost you about $50.

... The average pencil can draw a line 35 miles long and write about 45,000 words.

... Each year, in the United States, more than 225 million pencils are produced. There are more than 300 types of pencils made in 70 different shades and colors.

VOWELS AND CONSONANTS

See if you can translate the following sentence by inserting the missing vowels. (Vowels are a, e, i, o, u. All the other letters are consonants.)

_f _ll th_ p_nc_ls m_n_f_ct_r_d _n th_ _n_t_d

St_t_s __ch y__r w_r_ pl_c_d _nd t_ _nd, th_y

w__ld f_rm _ l_n_ l_ng _n__gh t_ g_ _r___nd th_

w_rld n_n_ t_m_s!

CURIOUS ABOUT PENCILS?

You learned something about pencils on the preceding page. If you answer all the following questions, you will double your knowledge and increase your collection of curiosities.

1. Why is a pencil usually referred to as "lead pencil" even though it is filled with graphite and not lead? (See almost any encyclopedia.)

_____

_____

2. Who invented the pencil with the attached eraser? (See Kane's *Famous First Facts and Records*.)

_____

_____

3. How much money did the inventor of the pencil with attached eraser receive for his patent? (See *The People's Almanac* by David Wallechinsky and Irving Wallace.)

_____

_____

4. There is no mention of a pencil in the *Guinness Book of World Records*. Dream up a pencil stunt that might get someone into that book.

_____

_____

5. A #1 pencil is soft (making a thick black line); a #2 pencil is medium (making an average dark line); a #3 pencil is hard (making a thin, light line). What ingredient is added to graphite that determines the softness or hardness of a pencil? (See almost any encyclopedia.)

_____

_____

6. How do Americans spell the past tense of the verb "to pencil"? (penciled or pencilled) How do the British spell the same word? (See any dictionary.)

_____

_____

7. At the beginning of this chapter, some functions of a pencil were listed. All of them are ordinary: that is, they are functions for which the pencil was designed. One unorthodox (unusual) function of a pencil is to stir paint. Can you think up *five* more unorthodox functions of a pencil?

_____

_____

_____

Now you know many of the *facts* about pencils. Go on to do some *thinking* about facts and pencils. Ready?

GRAPHIC THINKING ABOUT PENCILS

If you turn a fact into a picture, you can make it come alive! Which of the following sentences is more vivid?

A pencil can draw a line 35 miles long.

A pencil can draw a line from Albany, New York, to the Saratoga Racetrack, almost 35 miles away.

The second one is more vivid, isn't it? It uses specific details to make a fact come alive. Rewrite the same sentence, on the facing page, changing *Albany, New York,* and *Saratoga Racetrack* to two place names in your area.

→

Now rewrite the following sentences to make them more vivid, more exciting.

→

1. A pencil can write about 45,000 words.
2. A single pencil, if you made it yourself, would cost you about $50.
3. Since the early 19th century, more than 100 billion pencils have been made and distributed in this country.

PSYCHOLOGICAL THINKING ABOUT PENCILS

Pencils are important to people—so another way to think about pencils is to think about people's attitudes. For example:

Most pencils made today are yellow. There's a good reason for this: people won't accept pencils that are green, or black, or blue! One pencil manufacturer distributed 500 yellow pencils and 500 green pencils to the same user. In a short time the complaints started rolling in: the green pencils were scratchy, they didn't sharpen properly, they broke more easily. The truth is that the yellow and green pencils were identical. But people aren't happy with the unfamiliar—and the unfamiliar means any pencil of a color other than yellow!

To help you get started, here are a few questions that will stimulate some psychological thinking. (To think psychologically, just consider how and why people *think* and *feel* as they do.) Write your answers on the facing page.

→

1. Why do most students want to have several brand-new pencils for the first day of school? (After all, a pencil that is *half* worn can still write for 17½ miles!)
2. Pencils, more than any other inedible object, are chewed. Why?
3. People who are usually honest will snitch a pencil from someone's desk without thinking twice about it. Why?

Now, choose any *one* of your three answers and write a paragraph, similar to ours about pencil colors. Remember: think psychologically!

→

GRAPHIC THINKING ABOUT PENCILS

Your rewrite: A pencil can draw a line from _____

_____

More rewrites:

1. _____

_____

2. _____

_____

3. _____

_____

PSYCHOLOGICAL THINKING ABOUT PENCILS

Your answers to the three questions:

1. _____

_____

2. _____

_____

3. _____

_____

Your paragraph about pencils and people:

_____

_____

_____

_____

_____

_____

_____

_____

_____

_____

_____

A FORMULA PARAGRAPH

Can you imagine what a mess pencil-making would be if a formula didn't exist? The 40 raw materials and 125 manufacturing steps could result in almost anything! Writing a paragraph isn't exactly like making a pencil. Most of the time, a formula isn't necessary or even desirable. But occasionally, following a formula will help you to write different, more varied paragraphs.

Here's one formula for a five-sentence paragraph:

> Sentence 1: interrogative sentence
> 2: declarative
> 3: declarative
> 4: exclamatory
> 5: declarative

This paragraph follows the formula.

> [1]When did the first pencil come into existence? [2]Probably it came into being thousands of years ago when an early ancestor plucked a burnt stick from the fire and doodled with it on a rock. [3]He must have been delighted with the strange marks it left. [4]Little did he know, on that long-ago night, that he was taking a long step toward civilization! [5]It makes one humble to realize that most of the great inventions came into existence in just this way—by accident.

Choose any information about pencils on pages 42 and 43 and write a paragraph that follows the formula.

Your turn $\longrightarrow$

A QUATRAIN QUEST

You've already written a *couplet:* **a two-line poem.** Now you're ready for the *quatrain:* **a four-line poem.** The easiest rhyme scheme is abcb. This means that lines 1 and 3 do not rhyme, but lines 2 and 4 do. Here's a light quatrain about chewing pencils.

> Whenever I chew on a pencil,   (a)
> The juices stir in my brain.   (b)
> Thank heavens for pencil-makers: (c)
> Without them, I'd go down the drain!   (b)

Try it. Take any idea about a pencil and turn it into a quatrain. Notice that the second and fourth lines are indented, and that the second and fourth lines rhyme.

$--\rightarrow$

Finished? Good. Then you're ready for something a little harder. This time take some information about pencils from pages 42 and 43; turn this information into a quatrain. Like this:

> In fifteen hundred and sixty-four,   (a)
> A storm tore up a tree.   (b)
> Graphite was found, right in the ground,   (c)
> And the pencil came to be!   (b)

Browse; select; write. Good luck!

$\longrightarrow$

A FORMULA PARAGRAPH

_____

_____

_____

_____

_____

_____

_____

_____

_____

_____

_____

_____

_____

_____

_____

_____

A QUATRAIN QUEST

_____

_____

_____

_____

_____

_____

8. DICTIONARY DAZE?

A dictionary is a curious thing: it is filled with words—yet it doesn't tell a story, or describe a situation, or explain a process.

It is not a science book—yet it can tell you what vaccination means, who Osler was, and what a nuclear reactor is used for.

It is not a math book—yet it can tell you the difference between a sine and a cosine, can teach you to do subtraction, and can tell you more about numbers than most math books do.

It is not a history book—yet it tells you who Napoleon was, explains the difference between a monarchy and a democracy, and provides the meaning and origin of "D-day."

A dictionary is not only a curious thing; it is *filled* with curious things, as you will soon see. Satisfy your curiosity by finding answers to the following questions, and let a dictionary be your guide! (Warning: the dictionaries we generally use are *abridged*, that is, shortened. To find some of the answers, you will have to consult an *unabridged* dictionary, one that contains *all* words in English and much additional information.)

1. Charlie used the word FIZGIG and you doubt there really is such a word. Look it up. Find two definitions and write them below.

   _____

   _____

2. Colors are hard to define. You wonder: how does a dictionary describe the color RED? Find out and explain.

   _____

   What is a RED HERRING? (Find *two* definitions.)

   _____

   _____

   How did the phrase, RED TAPE, come into existence?

   _____

   _____

   When and why did the RED CROSS begin?

   _____

3. You and a friend are having lunch in a restaurant. Your friend orders a spinach QUICHE. What is a QUICHE?

   _____

   How do you pronounce QUICHE?_____

4. You have a part-time job and your boss accuses you of BOONDOGGLING. About what is he complaining?

   _____

   What is the origin of the word BOONDOGGLE?

   _____

5. In swimming class, Sandy said she DIVED from the diving-board. Debbie laughed and said the correct past tense of dive is DOVE. An argument followed. Who is right?

_____

_____

6. Television westerns often are set in DODGE CITY. Where is DODGE CITY, what was it at one time, and what is its population?

_____

_____

7. What do GNOME and PNEUMONIA and MNEMONIC have in common? Look up all three and see if you can figure it out!

_____

8. Jessica says that GROUND is a noun. Bill says it's an adjective. Fred insists it's a verb. Who is correct? Prove your answer.

_____

_____

_____

9. Many people argue as to whether EITHER should be pronounced e th r or i th r. Which is right?

_____

10. You have been asked to collect for UNICEF and you agree. But you don't know what UNICEF stands for. Find out.

_____

11. You are preparing for a quiz show in which spelling is a category. Which of the following are correct? Spell the correct choices on the blank lines.

      ECSTASY or ECSTACY   _____

      MISPELLED or MISSPELLED   _____

      ATHLETICS or ATHELETICS   _____

12. Sometimes a word has a standard definition *and* a nonstandard definition. The nonstandard use is usually called *slang*. What is the standard definition of JAWBREAKER?

_____

What is the slang (or nonstandard) definition of JAWBREAKER?

_____

13. Usually it is easy to form the plural of a word. Just add "s" (lamp—lamps) or add "es" (class—classes). But some words like to be different! What is the plural form of the following words? Spell them correctly on the blank lines.

      HIPPOPOTAMUS   _____

      BANDIT   _____

      DATUM

USES OF A DICTIONARY

A dictionary provides *definitions*, or *meanings*, of words. This is one of its main uses. Examine the problems on pages 48 and 49 and see if you can find eight more uses of a dictionary—that is, eight other kinds of information a dictionary can provide.

Begin, on the facing page, with the words: "A dictionary can help you . . . ," where the main use is printed as a model.

Then list the eight other uses, starting each use with "to + a verb."

Example: "*to find* the definition, or meaning, of a word"

Some other possible verbs: *to discover, to learn.* (You may use a verb more than once.)

ONE WORD MAY HAVE MANY MEANINGS

One of the glories of our language is that one word may have many meanings. Consider the simple word THROW. It has more than twenty different meanings! For example:

1. "to propel through the air with a swift motion of the arm"
   Isaac picked up the ball and THREW it to Fred.

2. "to put on or off hastily or carelessly"
   As she entered the house, Dolores THREW off her coat and headed for the kitchen.

3. "to lose (a contest) purposely" (informal)
   Since he had won the first three games, Bob decided to THROW the fourth so that his little brother wouldn't have a temper tantrum.

4. "to bear (young) as cows or horses"
   At 3 a.m. the cow finally THREW her calf, and young Tim sighed with relief.

5. "to roll (dice)"
   I THREW a three and a two so I was able to advance five squares on the gameboard.

6. "to cast (a shadow)"
   I could tell by the shadows THROWN by the buildings that it was mid-afternoon.

7. "to put abruptly or forcibly into a specified condition"
   This will THROW you into a state of shock: you were just elected president of our class!

8. "to perplex or mislead"
   His arguments THREW me—I was more confused than ever when he finished talking.

9. "to move (a controlling lever or switch)"
   As Nancy entered the room, she THREW on a switch and the ceiling lights came on.

10. "to arrange or give (a party, for example)" (slang)
    When her best friend won the ice-skating competition, Alice decided to THROW a party for her.

It's your turn. Choose one of the words on the facing page. Select *ten* of the definitions given for your word in your dictionary. For each of the ten, write first the definition, in quotes, and then an original sentence using the word as defined. You may use any form of the word. Consider this a challenge!

(*The American Heritage Dictionary* was used for the above exercise.)

USES OF A DICTIONARY

A dictionary can help you . . .

. . . **to find the definition, or meaning, of a word.**

. . . _____

. . . _____

. . . _____

. . . _____

. . . _____

. . . _____

. . . _____

ONE WORD MAY HAVE MANY MEANINGS

strike   do   leg   run   set   Your choice: _____

1. Definition: _____

   Sentence: _____

2. Definition: _____

   Sentence: _____

3. Definition: _____

   Sentence: _____

4. Definition: _____

   Sentence: _____

5. Definition: _____

   Sentence: _____

6. Definition: _____

   Sentence: _____

7. Definition: _____

   Sentence: _____

8. Definition: _____

   Sentence: _____

9. Definition: _____

   Sentence: _____

10. Definition: _____

    Sentence: _____

THOUGHTS ON THE LETTER "N"

Some people claim that letters have personalities: that "S" is swift and flowing, that "G" is harsh, that "B" is abrupt and booming! Let's explore this theory. We'll work with the letter "N." You choose any other letter in the alphabet. $\longrightarrow$

The *first* step is to TAKE NOTES. A dictionary is essential. We found these interesting "N" words: nice, never, November, new, next, near, no, not, narcissus, necessary, neighbor, natural, name, newsy, nickel, night, neither, noisy, neurotic, nuptial, North, now, nectar, noble, need, nuts, nutty, nudges, number, nasty, neglectful, negative, never, nonsensical, necessarily.

List, on the facing page, at least 30 interesting words for your letter. $\longrightarrow$

The *second* step is to THINK. After studying our list carefully, we decide that the "N" words can be divided into two categories: (1) "N" is *Nice;* and (2) "N" is *Negative.* You find two categories for your letter. $\longrightarrow$

The *third* step is to WRITE.

Begin with two sentences that introduce your letter.	*"N" is a curious letter. It is Nice and Natural, but it is also rather Negative.*
Discuss the first category.	*"N" is warm. What is warmer than a Nice Neighbor? "N" is Near when you Need it, and Nudges you forward with Next. "N" is Newsy—and Now!*
Discuss the second category.	*But "N" is also No, and Not, and Never. Either gives a choice; Neither doesn't. "N" is Nasty and Noisy. November is bleak and Nickel is cheap.*
Begin drawing a conclusion.	*"N" is contradictory. It is Necessary yet Nonessential. It is Noble, yet Neglectful.*
Conclude.	*"N" is—let's face it—Nonsensical, Neurotic, and even a little Nutty!*

POSTSCRIPT ON THE LETTER "N"

Since you have collected many words beginning with the same sound, this is a good time to try your skill at alliteration.

> **Alliteration** is the deliberate use of several words beginning with the same sound: for example, *t*all and *t*owering *t*rees.

Here are two alliterative sentences.

"N" is ___nice___, ___newsy___, and ___natural___.
       (adjective)   *(adjective)*   *(adjective)*

It is ___necessarily___ ___noble___ and ___never___ ___noisy___.
    (adverb)   *(adjective)*   *(adverb)*   *(adjective)*

You try it—using your letter and following the same formula. $\longrightarrow$

THOUGHTS ON THE LETTER "_____"

Your letter: _____

Your words: _____

_____

_____

Your two categories: _____

_____

Your paragraph:

_____

_____

_____

_____

_____

_____

_____

_____

_____

_____

_____

_____

_____

_____

_____

_____

_____

_____

POSTSCRIPT ON THE LETTER "_____"

"_____" is _____, _____, and _____.
          (adjective)   *(adjective)*   *(adjective)*

It is _____ _____ and _____ _____.
   (adverb)   *(adjective)*   *(adverb)*   *(adjective)*

9. COMICS CARROUSEL

"America is a happy-ending nation," Dore Schary once said.

Maybe that's why the comic strip is America's favorite reading; for in the comics, good triumphs over evil, the powerful help the weak—everything turns out *right*.

1 ... The leading comic strips have a huge audience. *Blondie*, for example, appears in more than 1200 papers throughout the world, is read by fifty million people daily, and is read as many as seventeen *billion* times each year!

2 ... A 1962 survey found that 100 million Americans read the comic strips regularly.

3 ... During a newspaper strike, children and adults missed the comics so much that Fiorello LaGuardia, then mayor of New York City, read the funnies over the air.

4 ... At one time Dagwood and Blondie couldn't decide what to name their second child. More than 400,000 readers cared enough to write and offer suggestions!

5 ... In Crystal City, Texas, a statue of Popeye the Sailorman was erected—thanking that comic strip character for making Americans conscious of spinach.

6 ... Favorite comic strips include—Blondie, Beetle Bailey, Peanuts, Winnie Winkle, Gasoline Alley, Superman, Popeye, Orphan Annie, Dick Tracy, Terry and the Pirates, Dennis the Menace, Krazy Kat, Mickey Mouse, Flash Gordon, Buck Rogers, Prince Valiant, Li'l Abner, Katzenjammer Kids, Donald Duck, Smitty, Moon Mullins, Archie, and Pogo.

7 ... During World War II, Skeezix (Gasoline Alley) was scheduled to be hit by a Japanese bullet. Readers were so upset that the Pittsburgh *Post-Gazette* promised, in front-page headlines, that Skeezix would be all right.

8 ... Also, during World War II, Mussolini banned all American comics from Italy— except his own favorite, Mickey Mouse.

9 ... From 1940 to 1945, comic books were used as instruction manuals by the United States Armed Services.

10 ... In 1969 NASA selected Snoopy as the name for the Lunar Excursion Module on the Apollo 10 flight to the moon.

11 ... Some years ago Andy Gump ran for Congress. In the real election that followed, thousands of people wrote in his name, trying to elect this comic strip character to Congress.

12 ... Who reads comics? Practically everybody ... adults as well as kids, the college educated as well as people with little education.

COMIC STRIP CHARACTERS

B_ _tl_ B_ _l_y   P_ _n_ts

Bl_nd_ _   S_ p_rm_n

T_rz_n   D_ck Tr_cy

VOCABULARY FOR THE COMIC STRIP

Three writing techniques are especially popular with the writers and artists who create comic strips. You probably enjoy reading the comics. Knowing and understanding these techniques will help you enjoy them even more.

Technique #1: ALLITERATION

As you already know, *alliteration* **is the repetition of initial sounds:**

like *b*ig, *b*lue *b*uzzards; or *c*ool, *k*een *c*ats.

(Notice that *k*een begins with the same sound as *c*ool, though not with the same letter.)

Below are the first names of ten comic strips or comic strip characters. Can you complete each name *alliteratively?*

Mickey _____   Hagar the   _____

Beetle _____   Donald   _____

Clark _____ (in *Superman*)   Snuffy   _____

Lois _____ (in *Superman*)   Katzenjammer _____

Technique #2: ONOMATOPOEIA

Onomatopoeia **is the use of a word whose** *sound* **imitates its meaning.** For example, BANG is onomatopoeia. It sounds like what it is: a bang! Here are some more onomatopoeic words: HUM, BUZZ, CRASH, ZAP, CRACK, BOOM, HISS, WHISTLE, CRUNCH, SCREECH, WHINE, CLICK.

Suggest an onomatopoeic word that could be used effectively in each of the following comic-strip situations.

1. An explosion occurs when a cook puts popovers in the oven. _____

2. Lightning strikes the main character. _____

3. A bee flies around a little boy's head. _____

Technique #3: PUN

A *pun* **is a play on words.** Sometimes it involves the similar sound of different words. Sometimes it involves different meanings of one word.

Question: What is *hair on the chest?* Answer: A rabbit (*hare*) sitting on a *trunk!*

You try it. Remember: think of the *second* meaning, not the first.

1. What is an *ice-cold pop?* _____

2. What is *foul language?* _____

3. What is a *switch hitter?* _____

4. What is a *peacemaker?* _____

THE WIZARD OF ID

"The Wizard of Id" is a popular comic strip by Parker and Hart. The strip below appeared in the Sunday newspapers on September 16, 1979. Read it. Enjoy it. Then answer some questions about it, on the facing page.

WIZARD OF ID by permission of Johnny Hart Field Enterprises, Inc.

THE WIZARD OF ID

1. Find, in the comic strip, one example of a *declarative sentence* and write it below.

_____

2. Find one example of an *interrogative sentence*.

_____

3. Find one example of an *imperative sentence*.

_____

4. Find one example of an *exclamatory sentence*.

_____

5. Find one example of *alliteration*.

_____

6. Find one example of *onomatopoeia*.

_____

7. Find one example of a *pun*.

_____

8. This particular comic strip is made up of ten scenes, called *frames*. In the fourth frame, the word "sire" is used. What does it mean in this frame?

_____

What is another, more common, meaning of "sire"?

_____

9. In the third frame, the word "drought" appears. What is a "drought"?

_____

How should this word be pronounced? _____

10. The *narrative line* is the plot, the story itself. In your own words, write the narrative line or story summary of this comic strip.

_____

_____

_____

11. The *punch line* of a comic strip is the line or picture that makes the whole strip funny. In this strip, the punch line occurs in the last frame. The wizard's question isn't really funny in itself. What makes it funny?

_____

_____

_____

There you have it—your first analysis of a comic strip! You won't want to analyze every comic strip you read, but an awareness of the techniques used will help you to enjoy them twice as much as you did before!

USING INFORMATION

On page 54 there are twelve pieces of information about comic strips. Each piece of information can be used in different ways—depending on a writer's subject.

For example: Suppose a writer wanted to discuss how important comic strips are to Americans. The writer would begin with a generalization:

Comic strips are of great importance to most Americans.

Then, to develop that generalization, the writer could use the following items from page 54: #2, 3, 4, 5, 11, 12.

All clear? Good. You try it with the generalizations on the facing page. After each one, list the items that could be used as supporting details. (Items may, of course, be used more than once.)

TO THE RESCUE!

Everybody has a favorite comic strip. What is yours? (1) _____

Now—here's your problem. Someone is trying to stop forever the publication of your favorite comic strip! Perhaps a group of peanut growers is trying to destroy *Peanuts*. Perhaps NASA is trying to destroy *Buck Rogers*. Perhaps some citizens named Donald are out to eliminate *Donald Duck*. What dastardly villains are trying to eliminate *your* favorite comic strip?

(2) _____

Next, consider motive. The peanut growers may feel that *Peanuts* is making fun of peanuts and costing them money. NASA may feel *Buck Rogers* is giving the public the wrong idea of space exploration. Citizens named Donald may feel that *Donald Duck* is making them look ridiculous and causing them emotional harm. What is the motive for your villain(s)?

(3) _____ _____

Next, consider your opponent's point of view. Does your favorite comic strip really harm anyone? Is any group or individual made fun of? Would readers be influenced?

(4) _____

_____

Next, consider your comic strip. What are some of its good points? Does justice always triumph? Does the underdog succeed? Does it probe into human relations? Does it talk about current events? Does it give unusual information?

(5) _____

_____

Finally, *should* your favorite comic strip be eliminated? Why, or why not? (You may want to consider here whether comic strips should influence people, and whether the influence exerted by your comic strip is basically good or evil.)

(6) _____

_____

USING INFORMATION

Generalization 1: Even Government officials and industrial executives read the comic strips.

Items to provide supporting details: _____

Generalization 2: Almost every comic strip has thousands of devoted fans.

Items to provide supporting details: _____

Generalization 3: War is serious business—and the comic-strip writers know it.

Items to provide supporting details: _____

TO THE RESCUE!

Ready to rescue your favorite comic strip? On the facing page you did some thinking and took some notes. You already have, therefore, a kind of outline or rough draft of what you want to say.

   Turn 1 and 2 into an introductory paragraph.
   Turn 3 and 4 into a second paragraph, discussing your opponents.
   Turn 5 into a third paragraph, defending your comic strip.
   Turn 6 into a fourth and concluding paragraph, giving your decision and the reasons for that judgment.

_____

_____

_____

_____

_____

_____

_____

_____

_____

_____

_____

_____

_____

_____

_____

_____

_____

10. "THE TEN MOST..."

List-making, as we've already discovered (Chapter 5), is a curious occupation. Making the list is fun; interpreting it—that is, finding out what it really means—is enlightening. Here are a few more opportunities for fun *and* enlightenment!

I. *The Ten Places You Would Most Like to Visit*

Where would you like to go? What would you like to see?

Another country? China? India? France?

A specific place? The Baseball Museum in Cooperstown, N.Y.? Disneyland in Anaheim, California?

Make up your list now. Take your time. Think. Then decide.

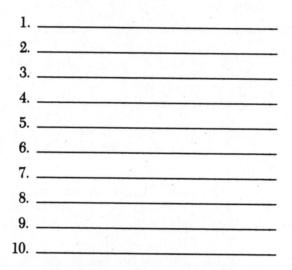

The Ten Places I Would Most Like to Visit

1. _____
2. _____
3. _____
4. _____
5. _____
6. _____
7. _____
8. _____
9. _____
10. _____

Before going on to II, look at the facing page. Read the questions and write down answers.

II. *The Ten People You Most Admire*

Whom do you admire most? A parent . . . a particular teacher . . . your best friend . . . a next-door neighbor? Choose *five* people you know personally, and admire.

Whom do you admire most in public life? A government official . . . a business executive . . . a singer . . . a baseball player . . . a doctor? Choose *five* people in public life that you admire.

Again—take your time. *Think*.

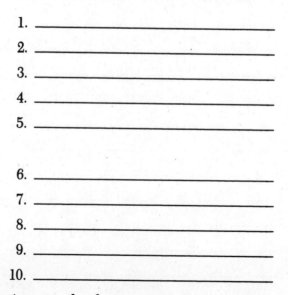

The Ten People I Most Admire

1. _____
2. _____
3. _____
4. _____
5. _____

6. _____
7. _____
8. _____
9. _____
10. _____

Before going on to III, look at the questions on the facing page. Answer them.

I. *The Ten Places I Would Most Like to Visit*

Asking questions—and answering them—will help you to interpret your own lists. Here are four questions. Answer each, using complete sentences.

1. Are *most* of the places on your list in this country or outside the country?

_____

What conclusion can you draw from your answer?

_____

2. Are most of the places specific locations (the Taj Mahal, for example), or general (Alaska)? _____

3. This is the key question, so consider it carefully. What do these ten places—or most of them—have in common? Are they exotic (unusual and marvelous) and a bit romantic? Are they connected with a particular interest, like sports? Are they places you have heard about from relatives? What common factor do they share?

_____

_____

4. Is it likely you will actually visit all these places during your lifetime? Half of them? One or two? None? _____
(Your answer to #4 will help you decide whether you're a romantic or a realist!)

II. *The Ten People I Most Admire*

Here's another cluster of questions for you to ponder . . . and answer.

1. What do you admire in each of the ten people on your list? Answer in one or two words—for example, enthusiasm, honesty, ambition, wealth, self-sacrifice, etc. Just list the qualities, not the names.

_____

2. Is any characteristic repeated several times? _____ Which one? _____
What does this suggest about *you*? _____

_____

3. If you had the chance, would you actually change places with any person on your list? _____ With which one or ones? _____

_____

4. How deep is your admiration? Answer each of the following by writing down a number. How many of the ten would you . . .

    . . . enjoy going out to dinner with?   _____

    . . . trust with an important personal secret?   _____

    . . . choose to live in the same house with?   _____

    . . . vote for, if a candidate for the U.S. Presidency?   _____

III. *The Ten Television Programs You Like the Most*

The Ten Television Programs I Like the Most

Include in your list specific shows: like "The Incredible Hulk" or "The Waltons."

Include categories: like the news or sports.

Include documentaries and specials.

Include movies, operas, ballets.

Include special specials: like coverage of Presidential elections, World Series, Olympics.

Include any or all of the above. Make up your list.

1. _____

2. _____

3. _____

4. _____

5. _____

6. _____

7. _____

8. _____

9. _____

10. _____

Before going on to IV, check III on the facing page.

IV. *The Ten Television Programs You Like the Least*

The Ten Television Programs I Like the Least

Consider all the types listed above for III.

You may find your dislikes fall into categories.

For example, you may dislike movies about war . . .

or award shows . . .

or game shows . . .

or children's shows . . .

Think. Make up your list.

1. _____

2. _____

3. _____

4. _____

5. _____

6. _____

7. _____

8. _____

9. _____

10. _____

Before going on to V, check IV on the facing page.

III. *The Ten Television Programs I Like the Most*

For I and II, we asked the questions and you answered them. For III, you ask *and* answer the questions. Try to develop four questions and answers about list III.

_____

_____

_____

_____

_____

_____

_____

_____

_____

_____

_____

IV. *The Ten Television Programs I Like the Least*

One more round. Again, you ask four questions about this list, and then answer them. Try to develop good questions: questions that point out how the various items on the list are similar or different . . . questions that indicate something about yourself as the maker of the list.

_____

_____

_____

_____

_____

_____

_____

_____

_____

_____

_____

What you have been doing in these four pages is—you have been making up lists, and thinking about them. You have been spotting similarities and differences among the various items on one list. You have been asking the question, "Why?"—and answering it. This type of exercise will make you a better writer and a wiser person, too!

V. *The Ten Things People Argue About Most*

In the classroom, at home, on buses, on television—wherever you go, you hear people arguing. (And sometimes *you* are one of the arguers!) What do they argue about? Think back about arguments you have heard in the last few weeks. Do people argue about money? Their children? Their parents? The high cost of living? You decide. What are the ten things people argue about most?

1. _____   6. _____
2. _____   7. _____
3. _____   8. _____
4. _____   9. _____
5. _____   10. _____

Next, ask yourself three or four questions about the above list. Answer them.

_____
_____
_____
_____
_____
_____
_____
_____
_____
_____
_____
_____
_____
_____
_____
_____

Some additional points to ponder. (You need not write answers to these questions, but think about each for a minute or two.)

1. Do people like to argue? Some people, or all people?
2. Is arguing necessary to human beings? Why, or why not?
3. Are most arguments friendly, or hostile?
4. What topics are most likely to result in hostile arguments?
5. Is there any point, any result to most arguments? Is anything gained? What would this world be like without arguments?

VI. *The Ten Things People Argue About Most (Continued)*

"Argumentative," as in "an argumentative person," means someone who likes to argue and often does.

"Argumentative," as in "an argumentative speech," means something that is full of arguments or disagreements.

Write a brief essay with the title, "This Argumentative World." Use your list, your questions and answers, and your ideas after reading *Some additional points to ponder*. Here is one possible organization:

Paragraph 1—an introduction to your topic
          2—a discussion of one type of argument
          3—a discussion of a second type of argument
          4—a discussion of a third type of argument
          5—a conclusion, a summing up

You may use the above organization, or one of your own.

"This Argumentative World"

_____

_____

_____

_____

_____

_____

_____

_____

_____

_____

_____

_____

_____

_____

_____

_____

_____

Notice how easy writing is when you have lots of material and have already thought about your topic!

TIME-OUT—II

I. Below is surely one of the biggest cookies in the world! It measured 18 by 22 inches and was baked by Judith Caplan.* It illustrates the song, "Twelve Days of Christmas," and does it in twelve scenes of various sizes. Below the picture is the last stanza, which describes all twelve scenes. The partridge in the pear-tree is depicted in the lower left-hand corner of the panel. Can you identify the other frames?

> The twelfth day of Christmas, my true love sent to me
> Twelve lords a-leaping, eleven ladies dancing,
> Ten pipers piping, nine drummers drumming,
> Eight maids a-milking, seven swans a-swimming,
> Six geese a-laying, five gold rings,
> Four colly birds, three French hens,
> Two turtle doves, and
> A partridge in a pear-tree.

Your job now is to design a very large cookie illustrating a favorite song or story. Where Caplan designed a cookie and baked it, you are asked to design a cookie and describe it in words, using at least six different scenes. Use separate paper.

Which song or story will you illustrate? _____

---

*From *Cookies and Breads: The Baker's Art*, by Ilse Johnson & Nika Hazelton, photos by Ferdinand Boesch. Copyright 1967 by American Craft Council. All rights reserved. Not to be reproduced in any form or in any medium without the prior written consent of American Craft Council.

II. You can play with alliteration, as well as work with it. Suppose your first name is Imogene. If you're feeling good about yourself, you might write—

Imogene: *imaginative, impish,* and *independent!*

If you're feeling bad about yourself, you might write—

Imogene: *idiotic, inconsiderate,* and *impatient!*

Your turn. Describe yourself alliteratively.

_____

Once more. This time describe your school *or* community, alliteratively. Example:

Merrydale: *memorable, metropolitan,* and *middle-aged!*

Yours: _____

III. You can also have a good time with graphic thinking. (See page 44.)

Facts: Two children ate 250 cookies in one week. Each cookie was about 2 inches wide.

Graphic expression: Two children ate 250 cookies in one week. That's *41 feet* of cookies, enough to stretch across some house lots!

You try it now.

Facts: Johnny rides his bicycle every day, seven days a week. He rides about six miles every day.

Graphic expression: _____

_____

_____

Facts: There are about 39,000 city blocks in the five boroughs of New York City.

Graphic expression: _____

_____

_____

Facts: The average person spends two hours a night dreaming.

Graphic expression: _____

_____

_____

Facts: Almost four human babies are born every second. That's 240 every minute, or 14,400 every hour, or 345,600 every day.

Graphic expression: _____

_____

_____

Words in Review

IV. Here are a couple of mini-crosswords on which to sharpen your word sense! Just start with a word you know; then build across and down. It's easy!

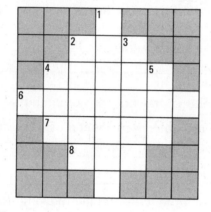

ACROSS

2. Prefix meaning "three"—as in
   _____cycle and _____pod
4. Litter, junk
6. Two-line poem that rhymes
7. Not this one—the _ _ _ _ _
8. A single, maybe, or a homer

DOWN

1. Described in vivid detail
2. The opposite of lies, even white lies
3. Small island
4. Also; more than enough
5. Objective case of "she"

ACROSS

1. Metal bolt used to join two objects
5. Tic-_ _ _-toe
6. Place where scientists work
8. To learn by memory, by _ _ _ _
9. Fastening made by tying string
11. False name
13. Nonstandard language
15. Weird, strange
16. Antonym of "wet"

DOWN

1. Unpleasant rodents
2. Frozen water
3. Large American deer
4. Light browns
5. Looks like a frog
7. What Superman is!
8. To free from the unwanted
10. Black, sticky substance often used in road repairs
12. _ _and behold!
14. New York (abbreviation)

V. COLOR KEY. Names of colors sometimes have second meanings. "Yellow," for example, names the color, but it also means "cowardly." Names of colors can also be combined with other words to form compound words: "greenhouse"—"goldfish"—"bluebird."

Equip yourself with a palette full of colors. Then "paint" a picture by inserting the correct color in each blank below.

Justin was _____ (despondent). It should have been a _____-letter day for him. After all, he had won the _____ ribbon and a handful of _____ backs for his prize-winning pig. And he was just a _____ horn, too.

But after the judging, everything went wrong. He got into a fight and received a _____ eye. He tried to snitch a cookie from the cookie jar and was caught _____-handed. He told a _____ lie to his father and ended up with a few _____ and _____ marks! If he had a little more _____ matter, he'd have the sense to run up a _____ flag!

VI. THE WIZARD OF ODD. You've already come across a couple of odd words—"fizgig" and "boondoggle." See if you can solve these problems and at the same time build your store of curious words. (Yes, it's all right to consult a dictionary!)

1. Peggy just tried to pick up her cup of coffee. It's too hot to handle. Does she need a "zarf" or a "tolu"? _____ Explain. _____
_____

2. For dinner Ken can't decide whether he wants some "quahogs" or a few "quarks." Which would you recommend? _____ Why? _____
_____

3. Someone calls you a "viator." Are you insulted or pleased or what? _____ Explain. _____

4. What would you expect to find in a "kiosk"? Newspapers, or sheep, or real estate agents? _____ Explain. _____
_____

VII. CODE OF VOWELS. Knights had a code of honor. You can have a code of vowels—for when you and your friends have secrets to swap. Just substitute punctuation marks for the vowels.

The Question Mark (?)	= a	The Semicolon (;)	= o
The Exclamation Point (!)	= e	The Quotation Mark (")	= u
The Comma (,)	= i	The Dash (—)	= y

Can you decode this? P?r!nts ?r! p!;pl! ?nd sh;"ld b! tr!?t!d w,th k,ndn!ss.

11. MONEY, MONEY, MONEY!

What is money, anyway?
It's whatever people want it to be—at a particular time and place.

> *Dried codfish was once used as money in Newfoundland,*
> nails in Scotland,
> salt in Abyssinia and Rome,
> corn in Colonial Massachusetts, and
> the teeth of sperm whale on the Fiji Islands!

... In other places and at other times, cocoa served as money, as did giraffe's tails, elephant hairs, bricks of tea, tobacco, and six-foot stones.

... In ancient Rome, copper pots were used as money. The word "copper" came from "kyprios," the Greek word for Cyprus, an island in the Mediterranean.

... In China, 2,000 years ago, metal shovels were used—until someone had the bright idea of making miniature six-inch shovels that served as well and were easier to carry around.

... In Africa, miniature iron spears were used.

... In this country, on July 6, 1785, the Continental Congress, by resolution, declared that the money unit of the United States would be the dollar. Our basic currency hasn't changed much since then—although its value has fluctuated!

... All kinds of coins are made at the Philadelphia and Denver mints, but only pennies are made in the San Francisco and West Point mints.

... A dime weighs 2.268 grams and is 17.9 millimeters in diameter. About 140 pennies weigh a pound.

... In the Philadelphia mint, 77 coin-striking machines work like cookie-cutters. Each one, in eight hours, can mint 140,000 quarters, or 250,000 nickels, or 300,000 dimes or pennies!

... Paper money is made in the Bureau of Printing and Engraving in Washington, D.C.

MAKE CHANGE

A wit once said that a quarter can still get you several things: pennies, nickels, or dimes! But if you know how to perform verbal stunts, you can get a lot more than that from a quarter. You can take away two coins (two letters) and get a unit of measurement: QUART. Or you can take away three coins and get a sad drop of water: TEAR.
Make verbal change.

1. Take three coins away from NICKEL and get frozen water. __ __ __

2. Take four coins away from a QUARTER and get a rodent. __ __ __

3. Take two coins away from a DIME and get yourself. __ __

4. Take two coins away from a PENNY and get a writing implement. __ __ __

5. Take two coins away from a DOLLAR and get a breakfast item. __ __ __ __

MONEY WORDS

So you think you know all about money, do you? Try this matching exercise! On the left are correct terms for money. On the right are slang terms. Match them!

(_____) 1. quarter   *a.* C-note
(_____) 2. $1 bill   *b.* peanuts
(_____) 3. $5 bill   *c.* two bits
(_____) 4. $10 bill   *d.* smacker
(_____) 5. $100 bill   *e.* dough
(_____) 6. $1000 bill   *f.* sawbuck
(_____) 7. small change   *g.* a grand
(_____) 8. money of any kind   *h.* fin

Here are some more slang or colloquial (informal) expressions related to money. Show that you understand them by inserting each after the sentence that best describes it.

nest egg   blood money   on the gravy train
well-heeled   payoff   penny wise, pound foolish

9. Oh, he has millions—more than he can ever spend! He's _____.

10. He won't spent a quarter for a cup of coffee, but he spends a fortune on gadgets. He's

_____.

11. They've been saving to buy a house. They call this money their _____.

12. The politician accepted a bribe. He took a _____.

13. He told the lynchers where his brother was and was paid off with _____.

14. She has a soft job and is making a fortune. She's _____.

DAFFY DIALOGUE

Because we're different, we often say the same thing in different ways. Consider, for example, the different ways of rejecting a frankfurter.

A whining child: "I don't want any! I hate it!"
A dignified adult: "Thank you, no. I prefer not to have one at this time."
A slangy teenager: "Nope." (or) "No way!"
A diet-conscious person: "That's full of calories! I wouldn't dare!"

Got the idea? Try it. Imagine someone asking four kinds of people for money. Mention the four kinds of people; then write the dialogue each person might use in answering the request.

1. _____ : _____
2. _____ : _____
3. _____ : _____
4. _____ : _____

BALANCING THE BOOKS

An accountant balances books; a writer balances words. Almost every sentence can be written in several ways, depending on the emphasis and the rhythm the writer desires. Here is an explanation of the phrase "stone broke."

1. In England centuries ago, if a craftsman couldn't pay his debts, the authorities broke the stone on which he worked.

The same words can be rearranged in a number of ways.

2. Centuries ago, if a craftsman in England couldn't pay his debts, the authorities broke the stone on which he worked.
3. If a craftsman couldn't pay his debts centuries ago in England, the authorities broke the stone on which he worked.
4. Centuries ago in England, the authorities broke the stone on which he worked if a craftsman couldn't pay his debts.

Now you try rearranging the sentence on the facing page. ———→

AUTOBIOGRAPHY OF A PIECE OF MONEY

Have you ever wondered what a penny sees during its "lifetime"? Or how a nickel "feels" about the many hands it has passed through? Or whom a dime has "met" during thousands of transactions?

Many coins and even some paper bills last a long time—years, even hundreds of years. Think of the experiences they have had! Think of the stories they could tell!

As you prepare to tell one such story, start by choosing a piece of money.

Our choice: a dime   (**Your choice**—on the facing page) ———→

Next, draw up an outline, like this one.

Paragraph 1: Birth of this particular dime—where, when, some details.

Paragraph 2: Dime given to a bank, then to a mother, then to her five-year-old son. Five-year-old played with it, chewed it, swallowed it. Lodged in throat.
Boy rushed to hospital. Dime extracted. Kept by surgeon.

Paragraph 3: Surgeon used dime in exhibit of things swallowed by children. Exhibit makes tour of elementary schools throughout country. Dime "sees" world.

Paragraph 4: Exhibit is broken up. Tourist puts dime in pocket of sports jacket. Visits Canada and uses dime to pay for coffee. Dime finds itself with Canadian dimes. Feels strange.

Paragraph 5: Store owner puts it in lion bank. Dime temporarily at rest. Glad for quiet period. Chats with other U.S. dimes. Wonders what the future holds.

It's your turn now, to draw up an outline. Notice that paragraph 1 is an introduction; paragraphs 2, 3, and 4 recount various experiences; and paragraph 5 draws a few conclusions.

BALANCING THE BOOKS

Here's your sentence to rearrange:

1. If you bank $10 a week at five percent interest compounded daily, after twenty years you will have $17,944.45 in your savings account.

2. _____

_____

_____

3. _____

_____

_____

4. _____

_____

_____

AUTOBIOGRAPHY OF A PIECE OF MONEY

Your choice (a coin or a bill): _____

Your outline:

_____

_____

_____

_____

_____

_____

_____

_____

_____

_____

_____

_____

_____

_____

You have an outline now, so you know the organization and content of the autobiography you are getting ready to write. You can concentrate on *how* you will write.

Begin by deciding the *temperament* of your piece of money. We decide that our dime is adventurous and curious, enjoying new experiences. We also decide that it will be a bit flippant, taking everything lightly, being amused at people and their world. You decide now what kind of temperament your piece of money has.   ⟶

Since the autobiography is supposedly being written *by* the coin or bill, you can see how important temperament is. This will determine *how* you write—even, to some extent, what words you use. O.K. Here's ours.

"Autobiography of a Dime"

I was born in the mint in Philadelphia on a hot July day in 1974. I weighed 2.268 grams and was 17.9 millimeters in diameter. 299,999 other bright and shiny dimes came into the world the same day I did. But I knew one thing for sure: *I* was different. I was no ordinary dime! I could hardly wait to start my adventures!

A few hours later I was tossed into a sack with a lot of my cousins. We were put into a truck and transported over some bumpy roads. In the morning I awakened in a bank. The teller gave me to a woman. "It's a bright, shiny new one!" she said with pleasure, and she handed me to Johnny, her five-year-old son. Johnny looked at me, squashed me in his fist, smelled me, stuck me in his ear, and bit me! I was about to scream for help when I found myself in a dark tunnel. Then sirens screeched and an ambulance took Johnny and me to a hospital. In seconds, a doctor pushed something into the tunnel and pulled me out. What a relief it was to see daylight again!

I owe a lot to that doctor. He attached me and some other things to a board with a sign: "Things Swallowed by Children." Then he took us all on a long trip. We visited elementary schools in Florida (it's nice and hot down there), in Mississippi and in Louisiana. Then we flew to California. The doctor took us out a couple of times on the plane so I did get a glimpse of the Grand Canyon and the Pacific Ocean. My new goal in life is to start at the top of the Grand Canyon and roll down all two miles of it to the Colorado River! Now *that* would be a trip worth getting tarnished for!

Back in Philadelphia, the doctor broke up the exhibit and I spent several months being passed from hand to pocket, from wallet to coin purse. Then one cold day in November, I landed in the pocket of a sports jacket belonging to a tourist. In Montreal, late that night, the tourist tossed me on the counter with some other coins in exchange for a cup of coffee. Next thing I knew I was with a bunch of Canadian dimes. *They* wear a picture of Queen Elizabeth, and I'd like to tell you they were a bunch of aristocrats! All I heard were wisecracks about royal blood and monarchies and upstarts.

But the next morning *they* were blushing! The owner carefully removed *me* and placed me in a small lion-shaped bank with some other American dimes. Believe it or not, I met three of my cousins there and we had a high old time exchanging experiences... not that *they* had anything very exciting to tell. It's quiet in here, but I'm glad to have some time to rest and to think. I wouldn't give up being a dime for anything in the world. And after I've rested a bit, I'll be ready for more adventures . . . maybe even for that long roll down the Grand Canyon!

AUTOBIOGRAPHY OF A _____ (continued)

The temperament of your piece of money: _____
_____

Its autobiography:

_____

_____

_____

_____

_____

_____

_____

_____

_____

_____

_____

_____

_____

_____

_____

_____

_____

_____

_____

_____

_____

_____

_____

12. "IN A PIG'S EYE!"

Consider the lowly pig.

A dirty and lazy animal, you say? Not so. It's clean, energetic, and aggressive, by nature. It's even lean, by nature. And—it's extremely intelligent! Isn't it curious how we misjudge even animals?

. . . Pigs have been around for at least 45 million years, and in all those years they have changed little. They still have 44 teeth and 14 ribs, interesting snouts, and cloven (split into two parts) hoofs.

. . . Pigs are prolific; they produce many offspring. Hernando de Soto, in the 16th century, took thirteen hogs to the Ozarks. In just three years there were 700 of them.

. . . Pigs are among the most dangerous fighters in the world. They can bite more ferociously than a lion, bear, or tiger.

. . . There are, today, about 520 million swine in the world, and about 67 million of them are right here in the United States.

. . . Pigs are omnivorous: they eat almost anything, including potatoes and artichokes, chestnuts and beechnuts, insects and earthworms. They also eat birds and small animals.

. . . Boars (male hogs) were used for centuries in Europe for "boar hunting." Their huge tusks and skilled fighting ability guaranteed an exciting hunt.

. . . Egyptians and Greeks used pigs to help them plant. The pointed hoofs made holes of just the right depth for grain seeds.

. . . Pigs formed the first primitive sanitation department. Allowed to roam the streets in Europe 500 years ago, they devoured scraps of discarded food and other garbage.

. . . Pigs can be taught to do tricks. In 15th century France, pigs dressed in pants and ribbons danced to bagpipe music to amuse King Louis XI. In 18th century London, a pig was taught to write words using letters printed on bits of cardboard. In the early 1900s, "Fred's Pigs" (21 of them) put on a vaudeville show, playing on a seesaw, climbing ladders, and balancing balls on their snouts. More recently, on "Green Acres," a TV show, one pig named Arnold Ziffel played the piano, carried schoolbooks and newspapers, received fan mail, and earned $250 a day!

PIG PLAY

You can be *almost* as clever as a pig if you can learn to change one word into another by changing one letter at a time. For example, you can turn a PIG into a DOG.

PIG—*jig*—*jog*—*dog*

You try it. Turn a SOW into a CAT, in just three steps.

SOW—_____—_____—cat

Now turn a BOAR into a LION, in four steps.

BOAR—_____—_____—_____—lion

A PIG VOCABULARY

Pigs are *porcine*—that is, they resemble pigs (naturally!). They have useful *snouts* (projecting front parts of their heads) which they use to *root* (dig up) food from the ground. They tend to be *rotund* (round, plump) and are short-haired. They are *prolific* (produce many offspring), and they are *omnivorous* (eat almost anything). They are easily *domesticated* (tamed; adapted to live with humans) and can be trained to come at their owner's call. This is why hog-calling contests have become so popular.

Pigs come with many names: *hogs* (when they are over 120 pounds), *boars* when they are male, *sows* when they are female, *piglets* or *sucklings* when they are babies, *shoats* when they are a few months old, and *swine* when they are in groups.

Select one italicized word from the paragraph above and use it in a sentence *not* about pigs.

Word: _____

Sentence: _____

CURIOUS ABOUT PIGS?

Root out some unusual information about pigs to add to your collection of curiosities.

1. What was the heaviest pig ever recorded? (See the *Guinness Book of World Records*.)

_____

2. How long was the longest sausage ever recorded? (See the *Guinness Book of World Records*.)

_____

3. Who first warned humans about "behaving like a pig"? (See Bartlett's *Familiar Quotations*.) Write down the quotation and the author.

_____

_____

_____

4. When does a pig come from a smelting furnace rather than from an oven? (See any dictionary.)

_____

5. What is "a pig in a poke"? (See Brewer's *A Dictionary of Phrase and Fable*.)

_____

6. Find out, in any way you can (books, other people, common sense), the meanings of the following pig phrases:

"to live high on the hog": _____

"to bring home the bacon": _____

"hog heaven": _____

7. Why is a *Duroc* (a breed of pig) called a Duroc? (See any unabridged dictionary.)

_____

STYLE A SENTENCE

In the preceding chapter you wrote the same sentence in several different ways. So you know a sentence can be styled. It's time now to be more specific.

The easiest kind of sentence structure is the SIMPLE sentence. Here is one. It has one subject, one verb, and expresses one idea.

> Pigs are omnivorous.

Using subject matter from the preceding two pages, write a SIMPLE sentence on the facing page.   **Your turn ⟶**

Compound **describes something with two or more parts.**

Use a subject of two or more parts in a simple sentence and you will have a SIMPLE sentence with a COMPOUND subject.

> *Insects* and *earthworms* are often eaten by pigs.   **Your turn ⟶**

Use two verbs and you will have a SIMPLE sentence with a COMPOUND verb.

> Pigs can *climb* ladders and *balance* balls on their snouts.   **Your turn ⟶**

Use two objects and you will have a SIMPLE sentence with a COMPOUND object.

> Pigs can be taught to carry *schoolbooks* and *newspapers*.   **Your turn ⟶**

Finally, combine two simple sentences, with separate but related ideas, and you will have a COMPOUND sentence. Connect the two with the conjunction *and*, *but*, or *or*.

> *Pigs are good fighters*, and *they can bite savagely*.   **Your turn ⟶**

CREATE A PIG

Your next job is to create a pig character: a pig that will make a fine hero or heroine for an animated television cartoon. When you have decided what kind of pig (or boar or sow or shoat or hog) you want, create an appropriate name.

> OURS: Puzzle Pig.   **Yours ⟶**

Next, describe the clothing your pig will wear. Use simple sentences with compound objects.

> OURS: Puzzle Pig will wear black-and-white checkered *overalls* (like a crossword puzzle) and a thin black *necktie* tied with five knots. He will wear a tall black *hat* and professor-like *eyeglasses*.   **Yours ⟶**

Next, describe what your pig will do. Use simple sentences with compound verbs.

> OURS: Puzzle Pig *will create* and *solve* puzzles. He *will sing* and *dance*. He *will solve* crimes and *capture* criminals.   **Yours ⟶**

Finally, explain the purpose or purposes of your pig-cartoon program. Use a compound sentence. Here are three simple sentences combined into one compound sentence.

> OURS: Puzzle Pig will teach pre-schoolers to do simple math, he will teach them a great deal about pigs, *and* he will, at the same time, keep them amused and quiet.   **Yours ⟶**

STYLE A SENTENCE

A SIMPLE sentence: _____

A SIMPLE sentence with a COMPOUND subject: _____

_____

A SIMPLE sentence with a COMPOUND verb: _____

_____

A SIMPLE sentence with a COMPOUND object: _____

_____

A COMPOUND sentence: _____

_____

CREATE A PIG

Name of your pig: _____

Description of clothing your pig will wear: _____

_____

_____

_____

_____

Description of what your pig will do: _____

_____

_____

_____

_____

Purpose or purposes of your pig-cartoon program: _____

_____

_____

_____

_____

THE STORY OF ___Puzzle Pig___

You should be ready now to describe *your* new television program. Read the sample description below, noticing carefully the comments on the left. Then, on the facing page, write about your program. Work with one paragraph at a time: that is, read our first paragraph and then write your first paragraph before going on to the second. (Use information from pages 76 and 77 to provide "meat" for your program.)

Introduce the program and its length.
Describe its audience.
Give its purpose.

"Puzzle Pig" is an animated cartoon that will be shown on TV every Saturday morning for one-half hour. It is designed for pre-schoolers. It has a multiple purpose: to teach children to do simple math, to teach them about pigs, and to keep them amused.

Describe the main character.

Mention other characters that will appear.

Puzzle Pig is the main character, and he will wear the same clothing each week: black-and-white checkered overalls (that resemble a crossword puzzle), a thin black necktie tied with five knots, a tall black hat, and professor-like eyeglasses. Other regular characters will include Elmer the Boar, Annie the Sow, the shoat Tim, and Daisy, a pretty piglet.

Have main character introduce self. Give a little information about pigs.

Set up a gimmick (ours is a crossword puzzle) that will open each program.

In the first episode, Puzzle Pig will introduce himself. He will point out that pigs have been around for 45 million years and are really quite smart. He will explain that he, Puzzle Pig, loves to solve problems and hopes the children will help him. A small crossword puzzle will then be televised, and Puzzle Pig, working with the studio audience, will solve it. A different crossword puzzle will begin each program. The first one will teach children the various names for pigs: hog, boar, sow, shoat, etc.

Set up a problem for the first episode.

Farmer Brown will appear, asking Puzzle Pig to help him plant grain. Puzzle Pig will show how his hoofs are exactly the right size to do the job. But when they arrive at the farm, two bags of seed are missing.

Start solving the problem.

With his snout, Puzzle Pig tracks the thief until he comes to the spot where the sacks are buried. He roots out one sack. "1" he announces. He roots out the second sack. "+ 1 = 2" he says. Back at the farm, Puzzle Pig plants the grain seeds, dancing as he plants, and singing a ditty about "1 + 1 = 2."

Add one more scene.

Next, Puzzle Pig finds the thief, a raccoon named Rollo. He scolds Rollo who promises never to steal again. Then Puzzle Pig, Rollo, and Farmer Brown sit down to watch the grain grow (which it does immediately!).

Set up a concluding scene.
Hint at what will happen in the second episode.

As the first episode ends, Puzzle Pig promises that he'll be back next week with Elmer, Annie, Tim, and Daisy to harvest the grain.

THE STORY OF _____

_____

_____

_____

_____

_____

_____

_____

_____

_____

_____

_____

_____

_____

_____

_____

_____

_____

_____

_____

_____

_____

_____

_____

_____

13. BUMPER STICKERS

Want to tell the world what you think? It's easy, and cheap. Just use a bumper sticker!

CHICKEN LITTLE WAS RIGHT

DON'T FOLLOW ME
I'M LOST

HAVE YOU HUGGED YOUR KIDS TODAY?

For a handful of pennies, you can "autospeak" to as many as 5,000 drivers a day. Now *that's* a bargain! And if you don't like any of the messages available, you can buy a bumper-sticker kit and make your own. All it takes is some writing skill and a bump of imagination.

What kind of message can you express on a bumper sticker? The answer is—almost any kind. Some are gloomy: after all, Chicken Little thought the sky was falling down. Some are humorous, like the second one above. And some are warm and loving.

But all are brief. Since "autospeak" messages are seen for only a couple of seconds, they must catch the eye and attention—*fast!*

ALLITERATION

You know what *alliteration* is—**the repetition of initial word sounds.**

BALD IS BEAUTIFUL

SOCCER SWINGS

Write a bumper sticker (using alliteration) . . . any topic.

ONOMATOPOEIA

You know what *onomatopoeia* is, too—**the use of a word whose sound conveys its meaning.**

IF I'M GOING OVER 50
HONK

GIVE A HOOT!
DON'T POLLUTE

HONK and HOOT are onomatopoeic words. Some others: ZAP, CRASH, BOOM, BANG, HISS.

Write another bumper sticker, this time using an onomatopoeic word.

PUNS

A *pun* is a play on words. One bumper sticker proclaims: PITCH IN! and shows some-one tossing a piece of paper into a litter basket. It's a play on the word PITCH. PITCH IN means to help. PITCH also means to throw or toss. So PITCH IN has a double meaning. Here's another bumper sticker based on a pun.

TEACHERS HAVE CLASS

Your turn now. Create a bumper sticker using a pun.

_____

SENTENCE STICKERS

No doubt you recall that there are four types of sentences: declarative, interrogative, imperative, and exclamatory. Below are bumper stickers that use each type of sentence. After each example, write an original bumper sticker of your own, using the same type of sentence.

DECLARATIVE: WARNING . . . I BRAKE FOR ANIMALS

Yours: _____

INTERROGATIVE: I'M REGISTERED. ARE YOU?

Yours: _____

IMPERATIVE: EAT MORE POSSUM. . . . or . . . PITCH IN!

Yours: _____

EXCLAMATORY: DOGS—LOVE 'EM AND LEASH 'EM!

Yours: _____

CURIOUS ABOUT BUMPER STICKERS?

Conduct an investigation. Wander through a parking lot, notebook in hand. Track down two bumper stickers that you find clever or amusing. Write them below.

1. _____
_____

2. _____
_____

A COMPLEX ART

You have just reviewed four *types of sentences*. But there are also several types of *sentence structures*. You have worked with simple sentences and compound sentences. Today, take a look at the COMPLEX sentence.

A *complex sentence* is really two sentences, in which one depends on the other.

Here's an interesting bumper sticker:

I'D ENJOY THE DAY BETTER IF IT STARTED LATER.

"I'd enjoy the day better" is a complete sentence. So is "It started later." But the second one *depends* on the first. The subordinate conjunction IF connects the two and shows the dependency. On the facing page, create a bumper sticker in the form of a complex sentence using the conjunction IF.   **Yours**———→

Another conjunction that can combine two simple sentences into a complex sentence is WHEN.

WHEN GUNS ARE OUTLAWED, ONLY OUTLAWS WILL HAVE GUNS.

Your turn: write a complex sentence using the conjunction WHEN.   **Yours** ———→

Still another conjunction that can be used in writing a complex sentence is BEFORE.

GET POLLUTION BEFORE IT GETS YOU! **Yours** ———→

"READING" A BUMPER STICKER

You can *read* a bumper sticker with your eyes, and you can "*read*" it with your mind. The latter means to understand it, to interpret it.

For example, the owner of a car with the bumper sticker, AMERICA: LOVE IT OR LEAVE IT, probably loves this country and doesn't want to see it changed. The owner of a car with the bumper sticker, AMERICA: CHANGE IT OR LOSE IT, probably loves this country, too, but believes it should be changed if it is to survive.

Here are a few more examples:

HAVE YOU HUGGED YOUR KIDS TODAY? The owner of the car with this bumper sticker loves children and is concerned for their well-being and happiness.

BEAT THE HEATING CRISIS, EAT HORSERADISH. This car owner is concerned with the energy crisis but also has a sense of humor.

TALK WITH GOD AND HAVE A HAPPY DAY. This car owner is religious and wants to help others become happy through a better relationship with God.

It's your turn now. On the facing page are several bumper stickers. "Read" each one, guessing what the car owner must be like or what the owner's purpose is.

A COMPLEX ART

Complex sentence using IF:

_____

_____

Complex sentence using WHEN:

_____

_____

Complex sentence using BEFORE:

_____

_____

"READING" A BUMPER STICKER

1. DOGS—LOVE 'EM AND LEASH 'EM!

_____

_____

_____

2. I'D ENJOY THE DAY BETTER IF IT STARTED LATER.

_____

_____

_____

3. GIVE A HOOT! DON'T POLLUTE.

_____

_____

_____

4. IF YOU CAN'T STOP—SMILE—AS YOU GO UNDER. (on the bumper of a large truck)

_____

_____

_____

5. OPEN MINDS SAY MORE THAN OPEN MOUTHS.

_____

_____

WHY BUMPER STICKERS?

Some years ago Senator Talmadge said that anyone who spent time on bumper stickers was spending time on trivia. Not so! Bumper Stickers are Big Business. No one is sure how many are printed each year, but most estimates suggest that the figure must be at least *100 million*. The Texas Memorial Museum in Austin exhibits a collection of more than 10,000 different bumper stickers, the earliest from 1948. At least one out of every ten cars bears a bumper sticker—and often a car that has one bumper sticker has two or even three.

All right. Bumper stickers are popular. But why? Dr. William Flynn, a Georgetown University psychiatrist, once wrote that bumper stickers are a form of personal expression. They permit people to identify with something without getting personally involved.

Others have said that bumper stickers give the average person a chance to speak out and to exhibit personality.

Your assignment now is to write an essay under the title, "Why Bumper Stickers?" Include your ideas about *why* people paste bumper stickers on their cars and *whether* bumper stickers actually influence anybody else.

Before you begin, it may help you to know that Willena Adams, a member of the staff of the Texas Memorial Museum, once stated there are four categories of bumper stickers:

> political,
> social or religious,
> humorous, and
> promotional.

We've already discussed the first three in this chapter. The promotional bumper sticker may be totally commercial (like THINK SNOW, put out by a ski shop). It may be patriotic (like FLY NAVY). It may be sports-related (like SOCCER SWINGS).

You may want to use these four categories (or types) of bumper stickers in organizing your essay:

> Paragraph 1: introduction and statement of topic
> 2: political bumper stickers
> 3: social or religious bumper stickers
> 4: humorous bumper stickers
> 5: promotional bumper stickers
> 6: conclusion and summing-up

Before you begin writing, think about your title: "*Why* Bumper Stickers?" *Why* do people paste them on their cars? *Why* do other people read them and remember them? Do they influence anyone's thinking? Ask yourself these questions as you begin *each* paragraph in your essay. And use lots of examples of real bumper stickers (those in this chapter and those you have seen) to support your ideas. You should end up with a fascinating essay about a most curious topic!

WHY BUMPER STICKERS?

14. BUYERS IN WONDERLAND

Where can you buy meat, skis, magazines, and pizza?

Where can you meet your friends, loll on benches, and just talk?

Where can you play electronic games and (sometimes) listen to your favorite music?

Where can you skate, nibble at frozen yogurt, see a movie, and admire trees and rock gardens?

The answer to all the above questions is—a modern shopping center!

Shopping centers have been around for thousands of years. The first modern shopping center was constructed in 1956 in Edina, Minnesota, to give shoppers a little protection from the frigid winters. Since then, they have been multiplying madly, and today there are 20,000 of them. Together they account for almost 50% of all retail sales made in this country!

What exactly is a shopping center?

Well, it may be a covered mall or a few stores gathered around a village green. It may be a cluster of stores arranged in an L, or a U, or an X, or a ring. It may even be a strip center: a street with stores on both sides.

It may contain half a dozen stores or a hundred. It may include restaurants, game rooms, offices, skating rinks, preschools, meeting rooms, museums, theaters, and exhibit areas.

It may sponsor summer festivals and all kinds of mini-events: the arrival of Santa Claus, fashion shows, psychic fairs, and telethons. It may have scheduled days for a Farmers' Market, and other days for Sidewalk Sales.

It may be a social center for the young or the old. It may be a last resort for families on a rainy Saturday. It may be an impossible temptation for the compulsive spender, and an alluring one for the lover of gadgets.

In short . . . since Americans love to look and buy, to congregate and talk, to eat and drink and play, the modern shopping center is a very practical kind of Wonderland!

PROVIDE THE PRODUCTS

Get into an appropriate mood by changing PARTS of shopping centers into possible PRODUCTS. Example: Drop a letter from STORE and get a flower. Answer: ROSE. (The "t" is dropped and the letters rearranged.) You try it.

1. Drop a letter from BOOTH and get foot attire. __ __ __ __

2. Drop a letter from RINKS and get a basin. __ __ __ __

3. Drop a letter from TABLE and get a piece of wearing apparel. __ __ __ __

4. Drop a letter from PLANTS and get a piece of wearing apparel. __ __ __ __ __

5. Drop two letters from DISPLAY and get a checkered fabric. __ __ __ __ __

6. Drop five letters from RESTAURANT and get camping equipment. __ __ __ __

A SHOPPING-CENTER VOCABULARY

There are *urban* (city) shopping centers, and there are *suburban* shopping centers. (The prefix, SUB—, sometimes means "under," as in subway, and sometimes means "near," as in suburban.) There are even *rural* (country) shopping centers.

Some shopping centers are *multi-level*. (The prefix, MULTI-, means "many"—so a multi-level shopping center has two or more stories.) Many shopping centers are *multi-purpose*: they have more than one purpose. These often include rail or bus terminals, auditoriums, and even hotels.

A *mall* is a shady walk or a street lined with shops, and closed to vehicles. A *covered mall* is enclosed with walls and a ceiling. An *arcade* is a roofed passageway with shops on both sides.

Many shopping centers have *kiosks*: small structures (often round) where you can buy pretzels, or have keys made, or purchase raffle tickets for some charity.

Most shopping centers have a distinctive *decor*: a decorative style. Some use skylights, trees, and rock gardens to suggest the outdoors. Some use small booths, striped awnings, and sidewalk cafes to suggest European towns.

Most shopping centers are *accessible* (easily approached) by autos and trains. Many are famous for their huge *sculptures*: figures and designs carved from wood, chiseled from marble, or cast in metal. And many have gigantic *murals*: pictures painted directly on walls or ceilings.

In recent years, more and more shopping centers have been drawing crowds by sponsoring *mini-events*. (MINI- is a prefix meaning "small" or "short.") Some popular mini-events are the arrival of Santa Claus by helicopter, a concert by a popular singer, a table-tennis tournament. One even held a dance: "A Ball in the Mall"; and another held a reception for the stars and audience of a local opera group.

Now that you know the words, cover the top of this page with another book and see if you can match Columns I and II below. Two of the words are new, but you can figure out their meaning from the prefixes.

I	II
1. accessible	(__) *a.* a design carved from wood
2. sculpture	(__) *b.* city
3. kiosk	(__) *c.* near or outside the city
4. multi-level	(__) *d.* a small or brief event
5. suburban	(__) *e.* a small booth where things are sold
6. mural	(__) *f.* easily approached
7. decor	(__) *g.* having many colors
8. mall	(__) *h.* copies in a smaller size
9. urban	(__) *i.* having two or more stories
10. mini-event	(__) *j.* a large wall or ceiling painting
11. multicolored	(__) *k.* a decorative style or scheme
12. miniatures	(__) *l.* street with stores on both sides

CURIOUS ABOUT SHOPPING CENTERS?

Put on your magnifying glasses and your thinking cap and become a Private Investigator! Investigate *your* shopping center. If there is no regular shopping center nearby, investigate a "strip" center: a street with stores on both sides; or even a large department store.

Stroll, notebook in hand, through the shopping center. Write results on the facing page . . . in complete sentences, of course.

1. How many stores or separate establishments are there?

2. What kinds of stores are included? Note about four. Then add a couple of stores you find especially interesting.

3. Are there seating arrangements that encourage people to rest and chat?

4. Is there music? Are announcements made via the loudspeaker?

5. Are entertainment modules (units) included? For example, is there a movie theater? An electronic arcade? A skating rink?

6. Are there mini-events that may properly be called entertaining? A concert group? Santa Claus? Tournaments of any kind?

7. Are there mini-events that may properly be called educational? A coin exhibit? A stamp exhibit? An antiques show?

8. Does your shopping center provide any community services? Meeting rooms? Classrooms? A preschool? A museum? Perhaps even a church?

9. What is the decor? Is there any one decorative style or scheme?

10. Are there any kiosks? What shape are they? What do they sell or offer?

11. Is there any landscaping? Gardens? Trees? Fountains?

12. Are there any sculptures? Any murals?

13. What kind of lighting is favored? Is the light bright or soft? Are there shadows?

14. Are the signs big and flashy, or small and dignified?

15. Are there any special exhibits or activities going on right now? What kind?

16. What kinds of people are using the shopping center? Young or old? Men or women? Which group seems to be largest?

17. Are most people in pairs, alone, or in groups? Are there teenagers "hanging out"? Senior citizens socializing? Families?

18. What is the *mood* of the shopping center? Are most people moving quickly to accomplish their tasks? Or are they window-shopping, chatting, and visiting?

19. Pause for a moment in one of the busiest sections of the shopping center. Describe what you see, emphasizing the various activities of the people. Be as specific as you can, noting even a crying baby or a woman overburdened with packages.

20. You have been observing and taking notes. Now, think. Why have shopping centers, and especially malls, become so popular? What do they offer that is different, that is desired by millions of people?

CURIOUS ABOUT SHOPPING CENTERS?

_____

_____

_____

_____

_____

_____

_____

_____

_____

_____

_____

_____

_____

_____

_____

_____

_____

_____

_____

_____

_____

_____

_____

_____

    You are now a mini-expert on shopping centers, and you should be ready to draw up
a blueprint for a totally original one—one planned just for *your* age group!

YOUR OWN WONDERLAND

Imagine a shopping center designed just for you and your friends! It certainly would be a *curious* one. And who is better equipped to design this shopping center than *you?*

First.   List (on the facing page) three special stores you would include. If you're fond of pigs, you may want a Piggery. If you're a soccer fan, you may want Socceroo!—a store devoted to soccer equipment, books, pictures, and instruction.

Second. List three kinds of entertainment that will be available, either regularly or on an occasional basis. Are you so crazy about roller coasters that you want one full-time? Do you want rock around the clock? Or a little theater?

Third.   Describe briefly the decor. Will you choose a nautical theme with anchors and sails everywhere? Or will you make it look like a gigantic discotheque?

Fine. You have some knowledge about shopping centers in general, and you have a few concrete suggestions for your own shopping Wonderland. It's time to create it.

PARAGRAPH 1: *Describe the physical appearance of your Wonderland.*

Start with a generalization.

Add details that support your generalization.

Give your shopping center an appropriate name.

The basic motif of my Wonderland is—white rabbits. The decor will follow this motif. There will be white rabbits holding signs, white rabbits welcoming visitors at every shop entrance. The floor will be green—simulated grass. The ceiling will be sky blue with hidden lights shining through it to resemble sunshine. A few live white rabbits will ramble freely, adding a touch of the unexpected to Rabbit World.

PARAGRAPH 2: *Describe the contents (stores, etc.) of your Wonderland.*

Again, begin with a generalization.

Add details that support your generalization.

There will be regular stores, of course: food stores, clothing stores, jewelry stores. But what will make my Rabbit World different from other shopping centers is three particular kinds of stores. There will be pet stores, each devoted to a different kind of pet. In the very center of the mall will be a rabbit store. There will be not one large electronic arcade, but a series of small arcades throughout the center. Each will feature one kind of electronic game. Finally, there will be Eat 'n' Exercise stores where you can eat a doughnut while biking away the calories!

PARAGRAPH 3: *Describe the mini-events of your Wonderland.*

Again, begin with a generalization.

Add details that support your generalization.

End with a sentence that is general and forms a brief conclusion.

There will be many kinds of mini-events. Every afternoon from 4 to 5, there will be a White Rabbit Concert, featuring local combo groups. Three evenings a week there will be electronic game tournaments with super prizes for the top winners. Every Saturday will be Stir 'n' Taste Time when *we* will have a chance to help cook and sample foods from all over the world. There will be something for everyone, making Rabbit World everybody's Wonderland!

YOUR OWN WONDERLAND

Three special stores you would include:

_____

_____

Three kinds of entertainment that will be available:

_____

_____

Brief description of the decor:

_____

_____

Paragraph 1:

_____

_____

_____

_____

_____

Paragraph 2:

_____

_____

_____

_____

Paragraph 3:

_____

_____

_____

_____

_____

Fun, wasn't it? Before you go on, look carefully at the three paragraphs you wrote. Did you vary the sentence structure? Do you have simple, compound, *and* complex sentences? If you did, good. If you didn't, go back and revise a bit right now—and try again in Chapter 15.

15. WEATHER

"Everybody talks about the weather, but nobody does anything about it."

—Charles Dudley Warner

All right. Let's talk about it.

First of all, there's a difference between weather and climate. *Weather* is the activity of the atmosphere on any particular day. It may be sunny, or raining, or snowing. It may be hot or cold or in between. When you add up 365 days of weather (rainfall, temperature, etc.) and get an average, that's *climate*.

One thing most people agree on: weather is unpredictable. You never know what's going to happen next! Here are a few curious weather statistics.

... On January 17, 1867, Dorchester, Massachusetts, had *five feet* of snow.

... In Potter, Nebraska, on July 6, 1928, one hailstone fell that measured 17 inches in circumference and weighed 1½ pounds.

... In Hastings, New Zealand, on July 13, 1949, gigantic waterspouts caused a "rainstorm" of fish—some as long as four inches in length.

... A hurricane along the New England coast in September, 1938, destroyed 13,898 buildings, 2,605 boats, and resulted in more than 500 deaths and 1,750 injuries.

... 1816 is called the "year without a summer." In the Northeast, there was a heavy snowfall in June and frost in July and August. In Connecticut, people wore overcoats on the Fourth of July!

... Weather twice defeated Napoleon. First the cold and snow abruptly ended his attack on Moscow; then rain frustrated his plans at Waterloo.

... In the 1930s, persistent dry weather turned the Southwest into a huge and unproductive Dust Bowl, adding considerably to the terrors of the Great Depression.

... Today, the United States and other nations maintain 100,000 stations to keep track of the weather in all parts of the globe. In addition, satellites keep track of the weather in over 4 billion cubic miles of atmosphere.

... On a smaller scale ... planning a picnic almost inevitably causes rain ... getting a new sled means there will be little or no snow in your area ... and scheduling an important activity will bring instant sleet at any time of year!

WEATHER—WILD, WINDY, AND WONDERFUL

The dictionary is helpful in finding alliterative adjectives for a particular kind of weather. RAIN, for example, may be RESTFUL, or RELUCTANT, or REFRESHING, or RECENT, or RAPPING, or RAMPANT, or RAGING. Select *two* kinds of weather (heat, cold, winds, sunshine, snow, or fog) and find *five* alliterative adjectives for each of the two. (Be sure that each adjective makes sense when linked with that particular type of weather!)

1. Weather: _____

   Alliterative adjectives: _____

2. Weather: _____

   Alliterative adjectives: _____

WEATHER WORDS

There are all kinds of weather. You should know that . . .

. . . a **deluge** is a heavy rainfall or flood, and a **drought** is a period of dry weather;

. . . **dew** is water condensed from the air, usually at night, which appears on cool surfaces; and that **frost** is frozen dew;

. . . **fog** is a cloudlike mass of condensed water vapor close to the earth's surface, and that **smog** is fog polluted by smoke;

. . . a **hurricane** is a severe storm with heavy rains and winds of more than 75 miles per hour, a **tornado** is a column of air spinning violently at speeds of more than 300 miles per hour, and a **cyclone** is a mass of rapidly rotating air;

. . . **humidity** is the amount of moisture in the air, and that people have a habit of complaining: "It's not the heat! It's the humidity!"

. . . that **hail** is rain in the form of small bits of ice or snow, and that these pellets are called **hailstones**;

. . . **cloud seeding** occurs when planes fly above clouds and dust them with dry ice or silver iodide thus (sometimes) making rain.

Select any two of the above words or phrases. Use each in a well-written sentence.

Word #1: _____

Sentence: _____

Word #2: _____

Sentence: _____

WEATHER SAYINGS

There's an old weather saying: "Green Christmas—fat churchyard." A *paraphrase* of that would be: "If the weather is mild at Christmas, if there is no snow, many people will die before spring." (A *paraphrase* **is a restatement in different words.**)

Below are several more weather sayings. Paraphrase each one.

1. "If March comes in like a lion, it goes out like a lamb."

_____

2. "April showers bring May flowers."

_____

3. "Till April's dead,
   Change not a thread."

_____

_____

4. "If there be neither snow nor rain,
   Then will be dear all sorts of grain."

_____

_____

WEATHER TALES

Everyone over the age of five has a store of weather stories. You may remember the cold so severe that your tears froze. Or the hurricane that swept your refrigerator out of the house and deposited it in the middle of the petunias. From your store of stories, choose *one*. Some possibilities: the longest rainy siege; the hottest day; the coldest day; a special spring or fall day; a hurricane; a tornado; a blizzard.

Our choice: a mini-tornado on June 2, 1978.   **Your choice** ———→

At five p.m. on June 2, 1978, the sky darkened and sudden wind began to whisper around the corners of the house. A minute later the whispering wind changed to a roaring wind. Trees bowed to the ground helplessly. Birds' nests were hurled out of pines onto the lawn, strewing half-formed babies among the twigs. Hailstones pounded the house, shaking the windows and rivaling the wind as noisemaker. The electric lights died. Trembling a little, we walked outside. The lawns were white, inches deep in hailstones. The roads were swift-running brooks. One side of our garage had collapsed, the debris tossed twenty feet in all directions. The huge green spruce out front had lost its top eight feet and looked like a beheaded giant. And everywhere were branches—tinder for a gargantuan bonfire. In five minutes it was over . . . except for the clearing up.

It's your turn now. Use plenty of details. Use different kinds of sentence structure, strong verbs, and powerful adjectives. Write *your* weather tale!

IT'S ALL IN THE WAY YOU LOOK AT IT

For most people, the weather is a favorite topic of conversation. One reason is its versatility: the same weather seems different to different people. Consider *rain*. Rain on a particular day may be welcomed by the farmer, hated by picnickers, feared by the owner of an amusement park, loved by firefighters.

You can create an interesting piece of poetic prose by just listing *detailed* points of view about a particular kind of weather.

RAIN

Rain . . .
A pair of lovers run barefoot in it,
Their faces open to the sky.
A family on a long-planned picnic curse it.
A farmer offers thanks for fields refreshed.
A five-year-old, with winged feet, leaps from puddle to puddle,
A mother of five sighs, and reaches for aspirin.
Motorists, slowed by shifting seas on Main Street,
Honk and shout and mutter bitter words.
A swimmer chuckles, willing victim of the war
Of salty wave and cold, fresh water.
A dog crouches in a closet.
An old man opens the door, looks out, then closes it again,
And returns to his chair.
Rain . . .

Notice the variation in line length, the occasional touch of alliteration, the use of graphic verbs. Now you try it, with snow or sleet, or sunshine, or clouds, or hurricanes, or fog.

WEATHER TALES

Your choice: _____

Your description:

_____
_____
_____
_____
_____
_____
_____
_____
_____
_____
_____
_____
_____
_____

IT'S ALL IN THE WAY YOU LOOK AT IT

_____
_____
_____
_____
_____
_____
_____
_____
_____

Everyone is on the move these days! We're a mobile people, and few live all their lives in the community in which they were born. In fact, one out of every five American families moves each year!

Your community is split. Half the citizens want to *encourage* new people to move in. They think it will be good for business. Half want to *discourage* new people. They think the population is large enough already. Which stand will you take? ⟶

Now that you know where you stand, your job is to write a report about the weather that will encourage *or* discourage prospective residents. You must tell the truth about local weather conditions, but you can, of course, employ a favorable point of view!

Here's one *encouraging* report on the weather in upstate New York.

Introduction, stating general position.	If the angels had been able to choose a place to live, they surely would have selected Merrydale, in upstate New York! During the four seasons, Merrydale experiences every kind of weather. The variety is infinite!
Summer, with emphasis on activities.	Start with summer. Our June is superb, delightfully warm, just touched by mountain breezes. July and August are hot, but seldom humid! Hikers fill the trails, and mountain climbers yodel from the peaks. Motorboats dart across Lake George; sailboats swoop and dance; swimmers test themselves against river currents. It's playtime in the North Country.
Fall. (Notice change of pace with the repeated "Think of . . .")	Then comes fall. Think of skies blue beyond blue, and swiftly moving clouds. Think of Delicious apples, dimpled red, and McIntoshes, solid and dignified. Think of millions of leaves yielding their green to brilliant orange, crimson, golden yellow. Think of the nip in the air that fills you with energy and makes you shout, "Here I come, world!"
Winter, with emphasis on activities.	Next is winter. You awake one morning to a white, white world . . . not to the gray slush of cities, but to crystalline beauty. Skaters imitate Currier and Ives; brave souls break holes in the ice and snatch the unwary fish. Winter is activity, hearty laughter, cold hands warmed at roaring fires.
Spring, deliberately placed last because it is the most attractive.	Last of all is spring. Spring doesn't creep up as it does in less hearty lands. It bursts upon us! One morning the snow is melting, the grass peers through white patches, the trees are tipped with buds. The air is almost warm. Bicycles appear, and roller skates. Joggers line the roads, and softball teams fill every field. It's spring!
Conclusion . . . emphasizing the variety.	This is our North Country . . . a land of constant changes . . . a land where the weather itself will never ever let you be bored!

If the report had been meant to be discouraging, it would have emphasized instead the killing heat of upstate summers, the sometimes rainy falls, the deadening cold and everlasting whiteness of winter, the muddy roads and potholes of spring! It all lies in the point of view! Proceed now—to *your* persuasive weather report.

WEATHER-WISE

Your stand: _____

Your report:

_____

_____

_____

_____

_____

_____

_____

_____

_____

_____

_____

_____

_____

_____

_____

_____

_____

_____

_____

_____

_____

_____

_____

_____

TIME-OUT—III

I. You are cordially invited to the Homophone Hop! *Homophones* **are words that sound alike but have different spellings and different meanings.** You can go to a SALE or go for a SAIL. You can feel PAIN or touch a windowPANE. You can take a PEEK or climb a PEAK.

Below are six puzzles. See if you can identify the pair of homophones in each puzzle. The first has been completed to serve as a guide.

A long *tale*   A long *tail*   Waiting for the _____   Waiting for the _____

A garden _____   A garden _____   A bad _____   A bad _____

Two on the _____   Two on the _____   To _____ a bike   To _____ a bike

ONE MORE WITH HOMOPHONES

Close up the Homophone Hop by writing three original sentences, each beginning with one of a pair of homophones and ending with the other. (You may use the homophones above or any others you can think of.)

For example: *Vain* she was as she looked at her new weather *vane*.

1. _____

2. _____

3. _____

II. SENTENCE STRUCTURE TOURNAMENT. Can you recognize a simple sentence? A compound sentence? A complex sentence? If you can, you can win this tournament! You win one point for each simple sentence you identify correctly, two for each compound, and three for each complex. Good hunting!

	Sentence Type	*Points*
1. Robert Ripley drew all his "Believe It or Not" cartoons upside down.	_____	____
2. If you are average, you spend about two hours each night dreaming.	_____	____
3. The first Sunday comic strip, in color, was printed in 1896.	_____	____
4. Adjuntas, Puerto Rico, has the lowest zip code, 00601, and Wrangell, Alaska, has the highest, 99929.	_____	____
5. When President Thomas Jefferson wanted to find a Secretary of the Navy in 1801, he used a classified ad.	_____	____
6. The Statue of Liberty's upraised arm is 42 feet long.	_____	____
7. The world's shortest alphabet is the Hawaiian with 13 letters, and the longest is Hindu with 47 letters.	_____	____
8. Someone gets killed or injured in 8 out of every 10 motorcycle accidents.	_____	____

Did you identify each one correctly? Is your total 14? Good. Then it's time to relax with . . .

III. RIDICULOUS RHYMES. A really good backbone is, of course, a FINE SPINE; and a brutal gem is a CRUEL JEWEL. Can you find ridiculous rhymes for the following?

1. Strange facial hair   . . .   a w_ _ _ _ _   b_ _ _ _ _
2. A girl from Switzerland   . . .   a S_ _ _ _ _   m_ _ _
3. A very popular automobile   . . .   a s_ _ _ _   c_ _
4. A container for jokes   . . .   a g_ _   b_ _
5. A hobo in a rainstorm   . . .   a d_ _ _   t_ _ _ _ _

Now try it in reverse. Dream up definitions for these ridiculous rhymes:

6. A CHEAP SLEEP: _____
7. A WILD CHILD: _____
8. SLOW SNOW: _____
9. A TRUTH SLEUTH: _____

Words in Review

IV. Another search for words! This time find thirty words by moving from left to right, or from top to bottom. Circle each word as you find it.

Below the diagram, as clues, are definitions. The number of blanks after each definition indicates the number of letters in the word you are looking for. Write the words on the appropriate blanks. (In some cases, the first letter of a word is given as an additional clue.)

S	C	U	L	P	T	U	R	E	S	O	W
T	O	R	N	A	D	O	R	E	D	M	E
A	M	I	N	I	A	T	U	R	E	N	A
T	P	P	O	R	C	I	N	E	C	I	T
I	L	A	S	P	C	A	D	A	O	V	H
S	E	V	O	W	E	L	O	R	R	O	E
T	X	M	N	I	S	L	G	M	O	R	R
I	M	A	E	G	S	U	B	U	T	O	U
C	I	L	A	L	I	A	S	R	U	U	R
S	N	L	U	R	B	A	N	A	N	S	A
K	I	O	S	K	L	I	L	L	D	A	L
J	A	W	B	R	E	A	K	E	R	A	W

1. Figures carved from wood or cast in metal S_ _ _ _ _ _ _ _ _
2. Small copy of something M_ _ _ _ _ _ _ _ _
3. Hard candy or hard-to-pronounce word J _ _ _ _ _ _ _ _ _
4. Decorative style or scheme D_ _ _ _ _
5. Country-like R_ _ _ _ _
6. Rain or snow or sunny or cloudy W_ _ _ _ _ _ _
7. A canine _ _ _
8. A color, as in _____ tape and _____ herring _ _ _
9. A false name A_ _ _ _ _
10. Will eat anything O_ _ _ _ _ _ _ _ _ _
11. Can be easily reached A_ _ _ _ _ _ _ _ _ _
12. Female pig _ _ _
13. A wind storm T_ _ _ _ _ _ _
14. Sets of numbers, facts about anything S_ _ _ _ _ _ _ _ _ _
15. Difficult; having many parts; a kind of sentence _ _ _ _ _ _ _ _ _ _
16. Prefix meaning "small" or "short" _ _ _ _ _
17. Resembling a pig P_ _ _ _ _ _
18. A or E or I or O or U _ _ _ _ _
19. City-like U_ _ _ _ _
20. Small booth where something is sold K_ _ _ _ _
21. Plump, rounded R_ _ _ _ _ _
22. Large ceiling or wall painting M_ _ _ _ _
23. Antonym of "well" _ _ _ _
24. American Society for the Prevention of Cruelty to Animals (abbr.) _ _ _ _ _ _
25. Group of stores under a common roof _ _ _ _ _
26. Homophone for "won" _ _ _ _
27. False hair-piece _ _ _ _
28. Antonym of "front" R_ _ _
29. Prefix meaning "under" or "near" _ _ _ _
30. Uncooked _ _ _

V. PYRAMID PLAY.   Find the correct word to fit each of the following definitions, insert them on the blanks at the right, and you will construct an "S" pyramid. Can you do it in five minutes?

1. The 19th letter of the alphabet.   —

2. Too; also (She liked the movie and — did I.)   — —

3. A female pig   — — —

4. A combination of two words: smoke + fog   — — — —

5. Long, projecting part of head   — — — — —

6. Having a single unit; sentence with one idea   — — — — — —

7. To import into a country illegally   — — — — — — —

8. *Near* the city but not part of it   — — — — — — — —

9. Hair down the sides of a man's face   — — — — — — — — —

10. Figures chiseled from marble   — — — — — — — — — —

VI. PICKING PREFIXES.   You are thoroughly familiar with the prefixes *auto-*, *tele-*, *sub-*, *multi-*, and *mini-*. If you insert one of these prefixes in each of the blanks below, the paragraph will make sense.

The _____-colored _____ marine surfaced. On shore a man in an _____ mobile peered through a _____ scope. "If I had seen this on _____vision, I wouldn't have believed it," he thought. Suddenly a hundred men emerged from the _____ way, each armed with an _____matic. From a _____-level store nearby came another hundred, each armed with a _____ (small) rocket. The man sighed with relief. "It's just Merrydale's Department Store again—putting on another _____-event!"

VII. COLOR KEY.   You can feel BLUE, or you can paint the sky BLUE. How many of the following BLUE words and phrases can you identify?

1. Award indicating "first prize"   — — — —   — — — — — —

2. A delicious fruit   — — — — — — — — —

3. An ocean fish good to eat   — — — — — — — —

4. A type of jazz usually slow in tempo   — — — — — —

5. Occurring rarely — — — —   — —   —   — — — —   — — — —

16. SWINGING SKATES

Cher and Penny Marshall both love it. So do Jack Nicholson and Cindy Williams and Ringo Starr and Lily Tomlin.

Toddlers try it, and oldsters take to it with glee.

Doctors recommend it, and orthopedists find it exceedingly profitable.

IT, of course, is S-K-A-T-I-N-G—on blades or wheels. For anywhere from $1.98 to $750, you can buy yourself a pair of skates and become a "free spirit." You can play hockey, dance, race, or just twirl in circles. You can swoop up walls and career off a skating park embankment. You can commute to school, wait on tables, or just mosey along on a lazy spring day.

. . . Ice skates have been around practically forever. The earliest had blades of polished bone. Roller skates are more recent, probably first made in the 18th century.

. . . Roller-skating is the fifth most popular sport among teenagers; and ice-skating isn't far behind it.

. . . About 28 million Americans skate in rinks each year, and millions more roll along in parks and on streets.

. . . Motorized skates are already available. You can roll along for 30 miles for one hour on a single pint of gas.

. . . In 1928 John Balazs of Ohio decided to skate around the world. He did the first 9,000 miles in twelve weeks.

. . . Ice-skating shows have long been popular. In 1936 the "Ice Follies" opened and played to 40 million people in twenty years. Next came the "Ice Capades" and "Holiday on Ice." The latter used a portable rink so performances could be given all over the country.

. . . The first mechanically refrigerated rink was built by John Gamgee in London in 1876. It was known as the "Glaciarium." The first in the United States was built three years later in New York City in the old Madison Square Garden.

JUST . . . SKATE!

SKATE is a versatile word. It is the "thing" you attach to your foot; or a fish (large and flat); or a person. You may be a cheap SKATE (a penny-pincher) or a good SKATE (an easy-going person). You may turn reckless and SKATE on thin ice.

Even as a combination of five letters, SKATE is versatile. You can make anagrams from it. (**An *anagram* is a word made by rearranging the letters of another word**.) SKATE, rearranged, becomes KATES, as in: There are four KATES at this party. Can you find three more anagrams for SKATE?

_____   _____   _____

You can also make three- and four-letter words from the letters in SKATE . . . TEA, for example. Can you find eight more?

_____   _____   _____   _____

_____   _____   _____   _____

A SKATING VOCABULARY

If you want to be a good skater, you should first do some *limbering-up* exercises: light exercises designed to loosen and stretch your muscles. These will make you more *agile* (able to move easily and quickly) and more *flexible* (able to bend easily).

Next you will want to learn some skating *techniques* (methods or procedures) and some skating *maneuvers* (carefully planned movements). Soon you will want to *improvise* steps (make up on the spot, without preparation), for *improvisation* is part of the fun of skating.

If you *synchronize* your skating to music (adapt it to the tempo of music), you will increase your *coordination* (getting your muscles to work together) and will become a *precision* skater: one whose timing is exact.

Select any two of the italicized words above. Use each of the two in a sentence about something other than skating.

Word #1: _____

Sentence: _____

Word #2: _____

Sentence: _____

CURIOUS ABOUT SKATING?

This time you're going to satisfy your curiosity in a different way. Choose *one* aspect of skating. Some possibilities: *the origin or history of ice skates or roller skates; rinks; the Roller Derby; ice shows; disco skating; hockey, ice or roller; Olympic skating; an ice-skating star like Sonja Henie or a roller-skating star like Bill Butler.*

Your choice: _____

Now try to find three curious facts or anecdotes about your particular subject by exploring . . .

> . . . encyclopedias,
> . . . *Guinness Book of World Records,*
> . . . Kane's *Famous First Facts and Records,*
> . . . *Readers' Guide to Periodical Literature,*
> . . . or any other reference work in the library.

Write your "discoveries" below.

_____

_____

_____

_____

_____

_____

_____

_____

SKATING SYNONYMS

SKATING is all movement: gliding, racing, twirling, tottering, and, yes, even falling! You can't hope to describe skating unless you have your own storehouse of synonyms and near-synonyms.

A *synonym* is a word that has the same meaning as another word.

You can find synonyms in dictionaries, but the best place to find them is in a book of synonyms—like Roget's *Thesaurus of English Words and Phrases*. It's easy to use. Just check in the index the word in which you are interested. You will find one or more numbers after the word. These refer to sections. Look up the sections indicated and choose the words that best suit your original word.

For example: under GLIDE, we find three numbers. In the three sections we find words like *shift, slide, slither, roll on, stream, stir, flit, roam, skim, skate, ski,* and many others. From these we select the ones closest to GLIDE: *slither, sweep along, roll on, skim, coast.*

You try it now. Look up RACE, SPIN, TOTTER, and FALL and find five good synonyms or near-synonyms for each. Write them on the facing page.

SKATING IN VERSE

There's a kind of poetry sometimes called *concrete poetry* **in which the words actually form an image or picture.** A few words about love might be written or typed in the shape of a heart. Some thoughts about trees might be typed in the form of a maple or oak.

It's a way of making words and images work together, and it's fun to do. A word of warning: it's habit forming. Once you start, it's hard to stop!

Here is a concrete poem about skating.

Notice that the positioning of the words mirrors the meaning of the words. When you write your concrete poem, you may want to write about SKATING . . .

as a confusion of the two feet,
as speeding around an oval,
as gliding along a river at dusk.

Better yet, dream up your own idea. Then write . . . and draw. ⟶

SKATING SYNONYMS

Synonyms for RACE: _____

Synonyms for SPIN: _____

Synonyms for TOTTER: _____

Synonyms for FALL: _____

SKATING IN VERSE

AN INVITATION TO A PARTY

Written invitations are back in style. After you receive an invitation by telephone, you may wonder: "Did Don say 1:30 or 2:30? October 4th or 5th? At his house or at his cousin's?" With a written invitation, you don't have to wonder! Just pin it to your bulletin board and you can check and recheck the information any number of times.

For this particular assignment, pretend you have unlimited funds to throw a super-duper skating party. Ours will be on February 14, Valentine's Day. When will yours be?

_____

Next, write an invitation, using the one below as a model.

February 1, 19___ ___

Dear Jenny,

Tell *what* and *where* and *when*.

Don and I are planning an exciting skating party for February 14th, and we hope you will come. It will be from 1 to 5 p.m. at our old farm on Merry Lane.

Start a description of planned events. (Notice use of action verbs.)

We will begin with ice-skating on the duck pond. (Don't worry—the ducks have agreed to vacate!) We promise absolutely smooth ice and a prize to the one who cuts the finest heart! After that, we will play a little ice hockey, then adjourn to the rink we had built just for this occasion. On roller skates we will twirl to disco music and swoop across the floor in our own Roller Derby.

Finish the description of planned events.

The third event is my favorite! We've built a twisting maze outdoors, with ice paths and cement strips weaving and interweaving. We boys will hit the cement on roller skates, while you girls glide along the ice on ice skates. As the music grows faster and faster, we will skate faster and faster. Doesn't it sound like fun?

Repeat the invitation.

Please come! The party won't be a success without you. And don't worry about skates—we have plenty of both kinds. Remember: February 14th at 1 p.m. Just skate right in!

Sincerely,

Dave

Before you begin to write, remember:

VARY SENTENCES.

USE ACTION VERBS.

INCLUDE, IF POSSIBLE, A TOUCH OF HUMOR.

AN INVITATION TO A PARTY

_____

_____

_____

_____

_____

_____

_____

_____

_____

_____

_____

_____

_____

_____

_____

_____

_____

_____

_____

_____

_____

_____

_____

_____

17. THE ROBOT REVOLUTION

In 1921, Karl Capek wrote a play about robots called *R.U.R.* In it, Capek coined the word "robot"—a mechanism that can work like a human, behave like a human, and even (to a limited extent) think like a human.

A robot revolution! That phrase used to make people shiver, for it meant metal monsters who gained power, turned on their human creators, and took over the world! But no more. Today it means something quite different: millions of robot helpers making our world more comfortable. Think of the robots already working for us.

> The thermostat in homes and offices controls the temperature.
> The toaster ejects breakfast bread when it is *just* right.
> The oven turns itself off at the desired time, and even cleans itself.
> Timepieces are self-winding.
> Doors of stores and office buildings swing open as someone approaches.
> Traffic lights change as needed to keep traffic flowing.
> Garage doors slip upward at the push of a button.

All these mechanisms are robots. All help to make this a better world. Your assignment in this chapter is to design a very special robot for a very special job! You may want a robot to take care of your household chores, or to keep the family car in running order, or to be your personal servant when you ski, or surf, or hike. *You* decide!

OUR CHOICE: a robot that will be programmed for gardening.

YOUR CHOICE: _____

NAME THE FELLOW

Just for fun, give your robot a name that is also a palindrome. **A *palindrome* is a word that is spelled the same forward and backward.** EVE is a palindrome; so is RADAR.

> *Our robot's name:*   AGIGA (from agricultural)
>
> *Your robot's name:* _____

BASIC ABILITIES

Our robot, AGIGA, can . . .

> plow the vegetable garden,
> plant seeds and seedlings in straight rows,
> irrigate as needed,
> weed (without pulling up the vegetables!), and
> harvest and clean fruits and vegetables.

What can *your* robot do?

_____

_____

_____

ROBOT WORDS

Naturally, you will want to master a robot vocabulary. These are words that everyone *should* know today and will *have* to know tomorrow!

cybernetics—study of the control processes (or brains) of biological, electronic, and mechanical systems

technology—the use of scientific knowledge in a particular industry

automation—the science and use of self-controlled machines

automaton—a machine (sometimes in human form) that moves or performs without human help; a robot

feedback—the results of a process that can change the process. (For example: a child touches a hot stove, burns her or his fingers, and learns not to touch the stove again. The burning of the fingers is "feedback." Today, some robots can also "learn" through feedback.)

remote control—the control of a mechanism from a distance, usually by radio or by electricity

programming—the listing of instructions for a computer. (A robot is **programmed** to do certain things.)

Select any two of the above words or phrases. Use each in a complete sentence.

Word #1: _____

Sentence: _____

Word #2: _____

Sentence: _____

CURIOUS ABOUT ROBOTS?

One way to satisfy your curiosity is to ask questions and then answer them. Develop good questions and detailed answers and you will learn a good deal about your robot.

Question: Can AGIGA learn through feedback, or can it perform only preprogrammed activities?

Answer: AGIGA performs mostly preprogrammed activities. However, using feedback, I hope to "teach" it to kill tomato worms.

1. *Question:* _____

   Answer: _____

   _____

2. *Question:* _____

   Answer: _____

3. *Question:* _____

   Answer: _____

ROBOT RUNDOWN

Robots have to be preprogrammed. Humans program themselves. Before writing about your robot, program yourself—by acquiring a store of related phrases and information. We'll work on this page; you work on the facing page.

A General Description: *See* your robot in your mind's eye: what it looks like, how it is equipped. Here's AGIGA.

> AGIGA is made of pale-blue plastic. It is four feet high and has jointed knees and elbows to permit easy bending of the legs and arms. The head is oblong, the face a television screen that enables me to see a close-up of any part of the garden. AGIGA's feet are large, and the soles are equipped with long raking cleats that continually turn over the soil.

$\longrightarrow$

Alliteration: Collect a few alliterative words appropriate for your robot. Since AGIGA begins with an "a," we collected "a" words: *alarming, amazing, ambitious, agile, agreeable, ageless,* and *adorable.*

$\longrightarrow$

A Description of One Trait: This time select one trait of your robot and mention it in a generalization. Then support the generalization with two or three specific details.

> AGIGA is conscientious. If seeds are to be planted two inches apart, it plants them two inches apart—not one inch, not three inches. If irrigation is on its schedule, it checks to see that each plant has been watered to a depth of four inches. If it is weeding, it extracts *every* weed, making no difference between the tiniest and the toughest.

$\longrightarrow$

Simile: Create one simile to help describe your robot. (**A** *simile* **is a comparison using "like" or "as."**)

> AGIGA is *as* conscientious *as* a gray squirrel storing acorns for the winter!

$\longrightarrow$

Dialogue: Create a conversation between you and your robot. Keep your own style of talking and give your robot a distinct style of its own.

Owner: AGIGA! Are there many weeds in the potato field?
AGIGA: There . . are . . 1443 . . weeds.

Owner: Can you pull them all out this morning?
AGIGA: AGIGA . . can . . terminate . . twelve . . weeds . . every . . ten . . seconds . . 1443 . . weeds . . in . . twenty . . minutes . . and . . three . . seconds.

Owner: What else will AGIGA do this morning?
AGIGA: AGIGA . . will . . mound . . potatoes . . terminate . . potato . . bugs . . irrigate.

Owner: Smart AGIGA!

$\longrightarrow$

ROBOT RUNDOWN

A general description of your robot:

_____

_____

_____

_____

_____

_____

_____

Alliterative words for your robot:

_____

_____

A description of one trait of your robot:

_____

_____

_____

_____

_____

_____

Simile for your robot:

_____

_____

Dialogue with your robot:

_____

_____

_____

_____

_____

_____

_____

_____

ADD-A-ROBOT

On an island in the Pacific, a government-run factory is producing specialized robots that will fill certain needs in this country. Your final job is to write to Roberta Robot, who manages the factory, persuading her to add *your* robot to this year's catalog.

Here is our letter recommending AGIGA.

2754 Maxima Drive
Merrydale, Florida 00000
January 3, 19__ __

Ms. Roberta Robot, Manager
Add-A-Robot, Inc.
Island of Robotia, Pacific Ocean

Dear Ms. Robot:

One of the major problems facing the U.S.A. today is food production for us and for people around the world. I have a possible solution: a new robot—AGIGA.

AGIGA is a backyard farmer. It should be made of pale-blue plastic that will stand out from the green background. It should be about four feet high and should have jointed arms and legs. Its face should be a television screen that will, at all times, provide close-ups of any section of the garden.

AGIGA will begin the garden in spring, turning over the earth with the long raking cleats on the soles of its feet. It will plant seeds at the proper times, in precise rows. It will keep track of rainfall and provide additional irrigation as needed. It will weed, pulling out more than 1400 weeds in twenty minutes! And finally, it will harvest, bringing to the owner's door baskets of clean red tomatoes and cartons of polished zucchinis!

I am certain that, with AGIGA's help, every family in America can grow enough vegetables for year-round use. The vegetables would be fresh and not contaminated with commercial fertilizers.

I am sure you receive many recommendations for specialized robots, but I hope you will give AGIGA serious consideration. It is as conscientious as a gray squirrel storing acorns for winter—and you know how well fed gray squirrels generally are! Please produce the amazing, agreeable, and agile AGIGA—and help us to solve our food problems.

Very truly yours,

Jim Jamison

Jim Jamison

ADD–A–ROBOT

Your letter recommending *your* robot:

_____

_____

_____

_____

_____

_____

_____:

_____

_____

_____

_____

_____

_____

_____

_____

_____

_____

_____

_____

_____

_____

_____

_____

18. IF . . .

IF is a curious word. It has only two letters, yet how could we survive if IF didn't exist?

It lets us dream. "IF only I could fly . . . ," we say longingly. But that IF stands firmly, reminding us that we can't. But suppose IF wasn't there . . . suppose we *could* fly. The advantages are obvious: we could wander around the sky, cover distances in a direct line, feel free. But how about the disadvantages?

If we could fly . . .

> taxes would have to increase to pay for traffic lights and police officers in the sky,
> collisions would take place with horrible results,
> birds would become our rivals instead of our friends, and might even attack us,
> burglars would swoop through our windows, even though we lived on the twentieth floor,
> trash would rain on our heads as litter-birds discarded candy-bar wrappers and soda cans,
> . . . and never, never again, could we look up to a spring sky to find peace and beauty and stillness.

What a grim picture! Thank heavens for IF!

You try it. Choose an IF ONLY of your own. IF ONLY I had a million dollars . . . IF ONLY I could do without sleep . . . IF ONLY I were a famous Hollywood star right now . . . What is your IF ONLY?

IF ONLY _____

Now eliminate the IF. Your dream has come true! The advantages are obvious. But what about the disadvantages? Have you thought about them? Project yourself into this dreamworld and consider the new problems you might have to handle. List some of them below.

_____

_____

_____

_____

_____

_____

_____

_____

_____

_____

_____

THE "IF" FAMILY

As you already know, IF is a *subordinate conjunction,* **a word that introduces a sub-ordinate clause.** The magic of IF is that it can suggest so many different meanings.

The Envious IF: Sometimes IF expresses envy. Your older brother is reluctant to take your mother shopping. You say (wishing you could drive):

"IF I could drive, I'd take you anywhere you want to go!"

Write an IF sentence that expresses envy.

_____

The Excusing IF: Sometimes IF provides an excuse for something we don't want to do. A friend asks you to collect money for a charitable organization. You say:

"IF I had the time, I'd be happy to do it for you—but I don't."

Write an IF sentence that provides an excuse.

_____

The Conditional IF: Sometimes IF permits us to make a condition. We say:

"IF it isn't snowing, I'd love to go with you to the mountains."

Write an IF sentence that specifies a condition.

_____

The Contrary-to-Fact IF: Sometimes IF expresses something contrary to fact. We say:

"IF I could see into the future, I'd know what decision to make."

Write an IF sentence that expresses something contrary to fact.

_____

The Cause-and-Effect IF: Sometimes IF states a cause, and the effect (or result) is in the main clause.

"IF I skate too fast, I'll probably fall."

Write an IF sentence that sets up a cause and effect.

_____

You have written five complex sentences, each starting with IF. And in each case, IF meant something a little different. A versatile word, this IF!

One more thing: after a subordinate clause, as in the model sentences above, there should be a comma. This makes the sentence easier to read. Check your five sentences above. Is there a comma after each subordinate clause? If not, add one. Good. Now go on to some more about IF.

IF AND IF'S COUSINS

More than half a century ago, Rudyard Kipling wrote a poem, "If." It's a serious poem, filled with good advice for young people. Here is the first stanza.*

> If you can keep your head when all about you
>   Are losing theirs and blaming it on you;
> If you can trust yourself when all men doubt you,
>   But make allowance for their doubting too:
> If you can wait and not be tired by waiting,
>   Or being lied about, don't deal in lies,
> Or being hated, don't give way to hating,
>   And yet don't look too good, nor talk too wise . . .

Because the poem is a bit preachy, it is easy to parody. (**A** *parody* **is a comic imitation that makes fun of the original literary work.**) Here is one example.

> If you can bowl and miss a strike and chuckle,
>   Or swing a bat and grin when you are out,
> If you raise just a racket with your racquet,
>   You're not a winner—just a darn good scout!

Notice that Kipling's rhythm is used and exaggerated—that the four lines of verse make fun both of Kipling's style and of the old saying that winning isn't important. Now you try it. Write two four-line parodies (or one eight-line parody) of the poem "If" about—school, or sports, or life with parents, or anything you wish.

IF'S COUSINS

You are an expert on IF, and it's time you met some of IF's cousins: other subordinate conjunctions. There are WHEN, and BECAUSE, and AFTER, and UNTIL . . . WHILE, SINCE, ALTHOUGH, and AS . . . UNLESS, WHENEVER, SO THAT, and more.

A little practice will sharpen your writing skills. Below are five sample sentences using different subordinate conjunctions. Opposite each one, on the facing page, write an interesting sentence of your own, using the same subordinate conjunction.

1. UNTIL I was fourteen, I believed that thunder was caused by angels bowling in heaven.

2. WHEN the Boston patriots rebelled against taxes in 1775, they didn't know what taxation would be like in the 20th century!

3. BECAUSE I am fond of skunks, I have invested heavily in spray deodorants.

4. AFTER the pirates found a chest of gold doubloons, they rushed to the newspaper office to place an ad in the "Lost and Found" column.

5. (An excuse for homework not done) WHILE I was studying last night, the Incredible Hulk crept into the house and stole my notebook!

---

*Excerpt from "If" which appeared in RUDYARD KIPLING'S VERSE: Definitive Edition. Copyright 1910 by Doubleday & Company, Inc. Used by permission of The National Trust, The Macmillan Company of London & Basingstoke, and Doubleday & Company, Inc.

IF AND IF'S COUSINS

_____

_____

_____

_____

_____

_____

_____

IF'S COUSINS

1. _____

   _____

2. _____

   _____

3. _____

   _____

4. _____

   _____

5. _____

   _____

POPPYCOCK PARAGRAPHS

"Poppycock" means nonsense. Here's a chance to work and play at the same time. Just write a few poppycock paragraphs in which almost every sentence begins with the same subordinate conjunction.

Silly Supposition

Begin with an "IF" paragraph. Try to end at the beginning! Sounds impossible? Read below.

> IF I don't close my eyes, I can't sleep. IF I don't sleep, I won't be able to concentrate in school. IF I don't concentrate, I won't graduate. IF I don't graduate, I won't be able to get a job. IF I don't get a job, I will starve . . . and all because I didn't close my eyes!

$\longrightarrow$

A WHEN Chronology

Next try a "WHEN" paragraph. Try it with hours of the day, or ages in life, or seasonal sports. Here's one on the seasons . . . by a lazy youth.

> WHEN the robin sings at dawn and I feel too lazy to go to school, it's spring. WHEN the sun is blazing hot and I lie in a hammock all day, it's summer. WHEN the west wind blows cold and I snuggle under a blanket, it's fall. And WHEN the snow reaches the window sill and I sprawl sleepily in front of a fire, it's winter.

$\longrightarrow$

The AFTER-Then Trick (useful when your mother asks you to dry the dishes)

Now try the "AFTER-Then" Trick. It's a bit like the "IF" Silly Supposition.

> AFTER this game is over on TV, I'll do my homework. AFTER I've done my homework, I'll feed the dog. AFTER I've fed the dog, I'll take him for a walk. *Then* I'll dry the dishes!

$\longrightarrow$

The Why-BECAUSE Syndrome

Finally try the "Why-BECAUSE" combination. It explains all sorts of difficult things.

> Why didn't I go to the class dance with Cliff? It's a long story! BECAUSE I talked in English class, I missed the school bus. BECAUSE I missed the bus, I had to walk home. BECAUSE I had to walk home, I was tired. BECAUSE I was tired, I didn't meet Cliff at the movies. BECAUSE I didn't meet him, Cliff was angry. And that's why I didn't go to the class dance with Cliff!

$\longrightarrow$

POPPYCOCK PARAGRAPHS

Silly Supposition Paragraph:

_____

_____

_____

_____

_____

_____

A WHEN Chronology:

_____

_____

_____

_____

_____

_____

The AFTER-Then Trick:

_____

_____

_____

_____

_____

_____

The Why-BECAUSE Syndrome:

_____

_____

_____

_____

_____

_____

You've had enough subordinate conjunctions, you say? Poppycock!

19. FAST FOODS

PEANUTS

© 1978 United Feature Syndicate, Inc.

In the comic strip, it is Charlie Brown who is in a hurry, and Snoopy, the customer, is not very happy about it. In real life, it is usually the customer who is in a hurry.

Some psychologists have called our time the "age of instant gratification." When we want something, we want it *now*. When we're hungry, we want to eat *immediately*.

One result is the fast-food restaurant.

The fast-food story began in San Bernardino, California, in 1948, with a single fast-hamburger restaurant called McDonald's. Thirty years later the Golden Arches straddle the country. Ronald McDonald, the restaurant clown, dominates parades and children's dreams; and the McDonald scoreboard screams: OVER 25 BILLION SOLD!

McDonald's is first in sales, but there are dozens of other fast-food chains: Howard Johnson's, Burger King, Pizza Hut, Lum's, Kentucky Fried Chicken . . . and more.

They have certain things in common: a limited menu, moderate prices, and fast service. They appeal to all ages, but especially to the young (who love the gimmicks) and to the old (who like the prices).

Fast-food restaurants have conquered the country, and now they're working on the world. In Japan, where the hamburger was almost unknown, McDonald's opened one restaurant, and by 1978 had 147! In every country on earth, people are chomping hamburgers and fingering fried chicken. So—it's really fast-food time!

PEOPLE FOODS

If he favors her, she's the *apple* of his eye. If he's skinny, he's a *stringbean*. If she's lovely, she's a *peach*. And if they're in love, they go together like *ham and eggs*. Try your hand at completing the following sentences by inserting the name of a food.

1. He has _____ ears. (battered)

2. She thinks she's the big _____. (more important than other people)

3. They consider themselves the _____ of society. (the top, the best)

4. She grew as red as a _____.

5. Because he has red hair, they call him _____-top!

6. They're as alike as two _____ in a _____.

7. Your new car is a _____. (sweet and smooth)

FAST-FOOD LINGO

If you hope to find your way around a fast-food restaurant, you should have an appropriate vocabulary. You should know, for example, that "turkey 86" means they're out of turkey! (This phrase began in a *not* fast-food chain, but a posh restaurant in New York. Each day the chef prepared 86 servings of the most popular dishes. When the 87th order reached the kitchen, it was greeted with a "Sorry, 86!") Here are some other fast-food terms:

the cow is dead—there's no milk left

zap it—put it in the microwave oven (and the oven is called a **zapper**)

Adam and Eve on a raft—poached eggs on toast

BLT—bacon, lettuce, and tomato sandwich

tuner down—tuna on toast

burn it—make it well done

let it walk—make it rare

with legs (or, **with wheels**)—order to be taken out, to go

sinkers—doughnuts

BLM—bacon, lettuce, and mayonnaise

grick bac—grilled cheese and bacon

coffee light—coffee with two creams

For some off-beat research, drop in at a fast-food shop in your neighborhood and see if you can track down two or three more phrases used by the employees.

_____

_____

CURIOUS ABOUT FAST FOODS?

Since fast-food restaurants are fairly new on the American scene, it's difficult to find out much about them through library research. So, start with *primary* research: talk to the people involved.

1. Go to a fast-food restaurant in your neighborhood. (*Don't* go during a rush hour!) Ask

   a worker: "What two items sell best?" _____

   Ask also: "What is *your* favorite item?" _____

2. Talk to some people who are eating at the restaurant. Ask three people of different ages: "*Why* do you enjoy eating at a fast-food restaurant?" Write their answers below.

   _____

   _____

   _____

3. Browse through a few cookbooks, at home or at the library. Try to find three unusual foods that seem easy to prepare and might appeal to a large number of people. Write them below.

   _____

   _____

A NEW BRAIN, A NEW CHAIN

Precisely because you're different from anyone else in the world, you should be able to dream up a new fast-food chain. Just start with some food that interests you—and let your ideas, interests, and attitudes shape your restaurant. You have one big advantage: you don't have to worry about going bankrupt!

The Specialty

Our specialty: the *soufflé* (pronounced SUE-FLAY), a light and fluffy baked dish
             made with beaten egg whites and other ingredients.   **Yours ⟶**

The Name: Choose a name that is catchy, one that is alliterative, that rhymes, or that just has a good, easy-to-remember sound.

Our name: *The Soufflé Shop.*   **Yours ⟶**

The Appeal: Everybody likes smooth, creamy foods. (Look at the run-away success of most ice-cream stores.) Soufflés are, by nature, creamy and smooth. They should appeal to everyone, but especially to the older diners who are increasing in number every day.   **Yours ⟶**

The Menu: Create a few basic items for your menu. Describe each briefly. Give the name and price of each.

Shrimp Soufflé, a basic main course—1.29
Soufflé D'Epinards a La Florentine (really a spinach soufflé)—1.89
Soufflé Heaven (ingredients are a secret!)—1.39
Strawberry Soufflé (should be the favorite dessert)—.89   **Yours ⟶**

Slogans: Write several slogans to be used in ad campaigns. Write #1 using rhyme; #2 using alliteration; #3 using any technique.

#1 Hot or cold, tart or sweet—
      The Soufflé Shop is hard to beat!   **Yours ⟶**

#2 Swing and Sway With a Sweet Soufflé!   **Yours ⟶**

#3 49 Soufflés! More Than Mother Ever Dreamed Of! **Yours ⟶**

Building Design: Describe the physical appearance of your restaurant. Be detailed. Consider using some symbolism.

The Soufflé Shop will be pushing Strawberry Soufflé as a delicious treat for any time of day. Since both Soufflé and Strawberry begin with an "S," the basic layout of the restaurant will be an "S" lying on its side. Employees will work in the long narrow S section. Inside dining rooms will be behind the S, and tables and chairs for patio dining will be in front of the S. The main building will be pink brick, the roof of strawberry-colored tiles. The large sign at the front of the building will be in the shape of a strawberry.
                                                   Yours ⟶

A NEW BRAIN, A NEW CHAIN

Your Specialty: _____

Your Name: _____

The Appeal of Your Shop: _____
_____
_____

Your Menu:
_____
_____
_____
_____

Slogans for Your Shop:

#1 _____
_____

#2 _____

#3 _____

Building Design:
_____
_____
_____
_____
_____
_____
_____
_____
_____
_____
_____
_____
_____

THE SOUFFLÉ SHOP

Your last assignment is to write a feature story for your local newspaper announcing the opening of your fast-food restaurant. It should be informative and newsworthy and written in a festive tone. Read the feature story below for The Soufflé Shop; then write one for your restaurant (on the facing page).

49 SOUFFLÉS!
MORE THAN MOTHER EVER DREAMED OF!
_____
Boasts Manager of New Local Restaurant

Headline.

Include the five W's: *What, When, Where, Who,* and *Why.*

A mammoth strawberry may startle drivers along Walnut Street today as The Soufflé Shop opens its doors for the first time. From 11 a.m. to 4 p.m., manager Jessie Lindstrom, and her staff of five, will offer soufflé tidbits, without charge, to all visitors.

A quote from the manager telling a little about the new restaurant.

"The soufflé is the food of the future," said Ms. Lindstrom. "They may be hot or cold, spicy or sweet—but they're always smooth and creamy—and, of course, so delicious!"

Background and reason for this site.

Ms. Lindstrom chose Merrydale as the site of her newest restaurant because she considers it "an up-and-coming town." She already owns Soufflé Shops in thirteen cities including New York and Chicago.

Local celebrity, plus a quote.

Mayor George Ellison of Merrydale will cut the ribbon at 11 a.m. and will be rewarded with a small plate of soufflé tidbits. Mayor Ellison said, "The Soufflé Shop will help Merrydale. Eventually it will employ more than a dozen people, and it will offer good, nourishing food."

Regular menu.

The regular menu will include 49 varieties of soufflé, including soufflés made with shrimp, spinach, mushrooms, tomatoes, cod, cheese and bacon, chicken, and chili. Dessert soufflés will include Chocolate, Orange Meringue, Apricot, and Vanilla Soufflés. Ms. Lindstrom's favorite soufflé, though, is the Strawberry Soufflé, made from an old family recipe. Mayor Ellison, who tasted it last month in Chicago, calls it "the food of heaven."

Schedule for the day.

Emphasis on "gimmick."

In addition to sampling soufflé tidbits, visitors may view a film study of soufflés and how they are made, tour the kitchen, and chat with Saucy Sally, the Soufflé Swinger. Saucy Sally is part of every Soufflé Shop and is a sort of clown-comic. She will present each young visitor with a balloon with a prize inside it, and with three nickel-sized chocolate-covered soufflé tidbits.

Regular hours. Final quote.

After tomorrow, The Soufflé Shop will be open daily from 10 a.m. until midnight. "In three months, Merrydale will be Soufflé City!" Ms. Lindstrom promised with a laugh.

_____ *(insert name of your restaurant)*

_____

_____

_____

_____

_____

_____

_____

_____

_____

_____

_____

_____

_____

_____

_____

_____

_____

_____

_____

_____

_____

_____

_____

_____

_____

_____

_____

_____

_____

_____

20. TIN CANS

Tin cans have a bad reputation.

They litter the countryside; they cause flat tires; they get rusty.
Anything that moves and rattles is called, with contempt, a tin can.
We toss empty ones, scornfully, into the garbage.

YET—surely the tin can is a most important invention. It makes possible long expeditions to unexplored territories. It accompanies mountain climbers and desert-crossers. It provides food for ordinary people snowed-in by blizzards or washed out by hurricanes.

It's a miracle, the TIN CAN . . . and most curious.

1 . . . In 1795 Napoleon offered a 12,000 franc prize to anyone who discovered an improved method of food conservation. Nicolas Appert went to work and in 1809 proved that he could preserve food in glass bottles. A year later Peter Durand took out a patent for tin vessels. And two years after that, Bryan Donkin and John Hall bought Durand's patent and set up the first cannery in England.

2 . . . In 1814 two British ships, the *Isabella* and the *Alexander*, set out for Baffin Bay. On board were "Preserved Meat" and "Vegetable Soup" canned by Donkin and Hall. For the first time a crew had an assured food supply.

3 . . . The word "can" is an abbreviation of "canister" and was used for the first time by a cannery in Boston in 1839.

4 . . . Directions on the labels of early canned foods read: "Cut round on the top near to the outer edge with a chisel and hammer." Today more than half of all American homes have an electric can opener.

5 . . . In 1824 Captain Parry of England outfitted a ship to search for a Northwest Passage. As provisions, he carried canned vegetables and meats. Two cans, one of roast veal and another of carrots, were taken back to England and kept until 1936. After 112 years, the cans were opened. The food was still good!

6 . . . The canning process is fairly simple. Food is heated to temperatures high enough to kill all bacteria, then cooled and sealed in airtight cans. In theory, food so treated should last forever.

7 . . . In 1974 more than 660 million pounds of tuna fish were canned—about 3 pounds for every human being in the United States.

8 . . . According to Robert Ripley (author of "Believe It or Not"), in the South Pacific is an island named Tin Can Island. It earned its name when a swimmer delivered mail between ships and the island. The mail was carried in—of course—a tin can.

TIN CANS EVERYWHERE!

Food comes in tin cans. So do tennis balls and jigsaw puzzles. Can you name at least two more unusual things that come in tin cans?

_____

When it is empty, a small tin can can become a cookie cutter, or even a child's bank. Can you think of at least two more unusual uses for empty tin cans?

_____

TIN-CAN WORDS

A TIN CAN is *hermetically* sealed: completely sealed. No air can get in or out.

Some foods are *vacuum-packed* in TIN CANS. The air is literally vacuumed out.

Once in a great while something goes wrong and food spoils. Eating this food can cause *botulism:* an often fatal food poisoning. Warning signs that food may be spoiled include swelling of the TIN CAN and rust inside the can.

In the 1840s TIN CANS were made by hand. Sixty cans a day was the *maximum* output of an expert craftsperson. (*Maximum* means "most," or "largest number.")

Those early TIN CANS were filled through an *aperture* (hole) in the top which was then sealed with a *soldered* disc. (*Soldered* = joined with melted metal.)

Americans added the *pictorial* labels to TIN CANS. A pictorial label is one with a picture on it. The first pictorial label showed a dish of red and green tomatoes.

In World War II, people were asked to crush empty TIN CANS and save them so they could be *recycled:* used again.

Select two of the italicized words above. Use each of the two in a well-written sentence.

Word #1: _____

Sentence: _____

Word #2: _____

Sentence: _____

CURIOUS ABOUT TIN CANS?

If you answer all the questions below, you will gain some curious (and useful) information. Check encyclopedias and dictionaries and any other reference books.

1. A TIN CAN isn't made of tin. What is it made of? Why is it called a TIN can?

_____

_____

2. What is "canned music"?

_____

3. What is the oldest canned food ever recorded?

_____

4. Why is an old dilapidated car called a "tin lizzie"?

_____

5. Why did the demand for canned foods increase in 1849 with the Gold Rush?

_____

6. "To can" means to place something in an airtight container. But "to can" also has several other meanings when used as slang. What are two meanings of "to can" when used as slang?

_____

_____

"CANNED" PREPOSITIONS

A *preposition* is a word that shows relationship. Combined with a noun, a preposition forms a *prepositional phrase*.

Once again, consider the TIN CAN. Something may be *under* the tin can, or *above* it . . . *near* it, or *on* it . . . *inside* it, or *outside* it . . . *by* it, or *beneath* it. Something may move *toward* a tin can, or *from* it. We may talk *about* a tin can, or *of* it. We may even speak *regarding* it.

Each italicized word below is a *preposition*, and each word group in parentheses is a *prepositional phrase*.

> (*Under* the tin can) is a pink satin tablecloth.
>
> (*Inside* the tin can) is elephant stew.
>
> (*Regarding* the tin can,) we can only say there are mountains of empties along every highway.
>
> (*On* the tin can) is a miniature but energetic giraffe.

On the facing page write *five* sentences, each beginning with a prepositional phrase. Start each phrase with a different preposition and end each phrase with the noun *can*. Make your sentences ridiculous or nonsensical and you will enjoy practicing this new skill.

TIN CANS AND COLLYWOBBLES

Isn't COLLYWOBBLES a fantastic word? It means a pain in the stomach—in short, a bellyache! Well, revising sentences about tin cans may give you a collywobble, but try it anyway. (Work on the facing page.)

1. Turn item 3 (on page 128) into one question and one answer.

2. There are three prepositional phrases in the first sentence of item 5 (on page 128). Just to prove how important prepositional phrases are, write the sentence *omitting* all three prepositional phrases. Does it make sense?

3. Combine the first and third sentences of item 6 into one compound sentence . . . that is, two sentences connected by the conjunction *and*, *but*, or *or*.

4. Combine the last two sentences of item 1 into one complex sentence beginning with the subordinate conjunction, *after*. (You will have to omit some words.)

5. In item 4, directions are given for opening canned foods in the 1840s: "Cut round on the top near to the outer edge with a chisel and hammer." Rewrite these directions in three different ways, using the same words but rearranging them.

6. Combine the last two sentences of item 8 into one sentence by changing sentence 3 into a prepositional phrase.

"CANNED" PREPOSITIONS

1. _____
   _____
2. _____
   _____
3. _____
   _____
4. _____
   _____
5. _____
   _____

TIN CANS AND COLLYWOBBLES

1. _____
   _____
   _____
   _____
2. _____
   _____
   _____
3. _____
   _____
   _____
4. _____
   _____
   _____
5. _____
   _____
   _____
6. _____
   _____
   _____

"CANNED" PARAGRAPHS

_____
_____

⟋⟍

These lines are parallel.   These lines are not parallel.

Parallel lines match each other: they go in the same direction and are separated throughout by the same distance. *Parallel sentences* **match each other, too. They go in the same direction, and their parts are related in a similar way.**

In Chapter 18 you wrote Poppycock Paragraphs. Now try some serious (and not so serious) Parallel Paragraphs!

Time Marches On: An easy way to use parallelism in writing is to start each sentence with a date.

> *In 1935* Jethro was born. *In 1940* he started school and was teased by the other children for his clumsiness. *In 1945* he could walk only with the help of crutches. Yet, *in 1955*, this same Jethro ran the mile in well under five minutes!

Now you try it. Write four parallel sentences tracing the history of the TIN CAN. (For information, see page 128.) Write the last sentence in such a way that a reader will say: "Wow! That's hard to believe!"   **Yours** ⟶

Again—and Again—and Again: Another way to use parallelism in writing is to use repetition. This often (but not always) results in humor.

> TIN CANS haunt me. I walk into the kitchen and find my lunch is to be tomato soup—from a TIN CAN. I crave a snack and grab some potato chips—from a TIN CAN. My hair is unruly so I apply hair spray—from a TIN CAN. I go out to play tennis and take along some new tennis balls— from a TIN CAN. No wonder TIN CANS haunt me and keep me awake at night! I wonder—have they canned sleep yet?

Your turn. Write a four- or five-sentence paragraph about TIN CANS, using repetition in parallel sentences.   **Yours** ⟶

If Only I Could Can . . . A few years ago someone offered to sell cans of fresh (unpolluted) air. The cans of air never sold as well as pet rocks had, but the idea is interesting. Suppose you could *can* anything in the world. What would you choose?

Our choice: a can (large, economy size) of spring air.   **Yours** ⟶

> If only I could can a little spring air! *When* the wild winds blow in November, I'd inhale the gentle breezes of May. *When* the snow gets inside my boots and gloves, I'd apply some June warmth to frostbitten fingers and toes. And *when* the temperature falls to zero and I shiver miserably and want only to die, I'd open the can full way and drink deep of hope and rebirth and lovely things. A can of spring air would certainly make a North Country winter a good deal easier to bear!

Use any kind of parallel structure as you write *your* "If Only I Could Can . . ." paragraph.

"CANNED" PARAGRAPHS

Time Marches On:

_____

_____

_____

_____

_____

_____

Again—and Again—and Again:

_____

_____

_____

_____

_____

_____

_____

_____

If Only I Could Can . . .

_____

_____

_____

_____

_____

_____

_____

_____

Before you go on, reread your three paragraphs. Aren't they smoother, clearer, more interesting than your writing generally is? You will want to use parallelism often. Just as parallel bars help when you are doing gymnastics, so parallel sentences help when you are writing!

TIME-OUT—IV

I. When is food not food? Enter the Dialogue Derby, and find out. First study the ten items of food below.

bread	egg
lemon	banana
molasses	apple pie
noodles	pickle
butter	piece of cake

Next, write a conversation between two people about some topic other than food. Include in each speech a food reference (usually a slang term) to describe someone or something.

Here's a sample, using several foods *not* listed above.

Jane: You're *crackers*, Joe! You know I can't go out tonight. I have to study.
Joe: That's a lot of *applesauce!*
Jane: It isn't. I'm really in a *jam* this time.
Joe: *Nuts!* You know you're the *apple* of my eye, Jane. I really want to see this movie with you.

Your turn. Can you use all *ten* foods listed above in your Dialogue Derby?

_____

_____

_____

_____

_____

_____

_____

_____

_____

_____

_____

_____

_____

_____

_____

_____

II. JIGSAW PUZZLE SENTENCES.
You've probably put together dozens—maybe hundreds—of jigsaw puzzles. Here's a chance to try something a bit different: to put together a jigsaw puzzle sentence. Start with the eight "pieces" listed below.

Nouns: Jack—Jill
Verb: showered
Adjectives: green and majestic
Adverb: joyfully
Prepositional Phrases: on certain hilltops—with flowers—of varying sizes and colors

Now arrange the eight pieces to make a good sentence.

_____
_____
_____

Fine, but here's something you *can't* do with a regular jigsaw puzzle! Rearrange the eight pieces again, in a different way, to make a different sentence.

_____
_____
_____

Rearrange them once more, to make a third sentence.

_____
_____
_____

Now *that* is a versatile jigsaw puzzle!

III. CLAUSE-AND-EFFECT.
You claim you have a good imagination? Prove it! Below are three introductory subordinate clauses. Add a main clause (italicized below) that will complete each sentence *and* amuse a reader.

Example: If hamburgers could talk, *they would surely charge fast-food restaurants with brutality.*

1. Whenever a robot enters the room, _____.
2. Although pigs are intelligent, _____.
3. Before you throw away all those tin cans, _____.

No, you're not finished yet! This time, try it in reverse. We'll give you three main clauses. You fill in three introductory subordinate clauses.

4. _____, *I fall asleep.*
5. _____, *only a few have succeeded.*
6. _____, *she cried bitterly.*

Words in Review

IV. There's a new game in town—called COLLYWOBBLES. You get to read the riddles (and chuckle at them) IF you can find them! For the first one, simply figure out the seventeen words defined in the list; then insert each word in the appropriately numbered blank.

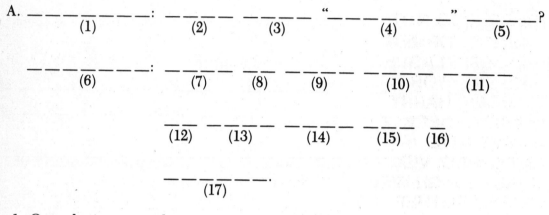

A. _ _ _ _ _ _ _ : _ _ _ _ _ _ _ "_ _ _ _ _ _" _ _ _ _ ?
    (1)   (2)   (3)   (4)   (5)

_ _ _ _ _ _ : _ _ _ _ _ _ _ _ _ _ _ _ _ _ _ _
   (6)   (7)   (8)   (9)   (10)   (11)

_ _ _ _ _ _ _ _ _ _ _ _ _
 (12)   (13)   (14)   (15) (16)

_ _ _ _ _ _ .
    (17)

1. One who instructs others.
2. _____ is a tin can made of? Answer: steel plated with tin.
3. Female deer (plural)
4. The average weather of an area
5. Stingy; malicious
6. One who attends school
7. An adjective: I want _____ robot, not this one.
8. Abbreviation of "island"
9. Who, which, when, where, _____

10. Maximum
11. Young goats or young children
12. _____, re, mi, fa, sol, la, ti, _____
13. At what time?
14. I laugh, you laugh, he, she, or it laughs; we laugh, you laugh, _____ laugh
15. Homophone of "sea"
16. First letter of the alphabet
17. Two long pieces of wood or steel crossed by parallel rungs

Try one more collywobble:

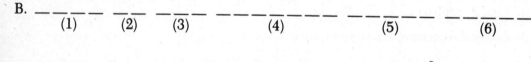

B. _
   (1)   (2)   (3)   (4)   (5)   (6)

_ _ _ _ _ _ _ _ _ _ _ _ _ _ _ _ ?
  (7)   (8)   (9)   (10)

Answer: _ _ _ _ _ _ _ _ _ _ _ .
          (11)   (12)

1. Which thing?
2. I am, you are, he, she, or it _____
3. Definite article, as in "Jack and Jill went up _____ hill"
4. Most difficult
5. Any _____, every _____, no _____
6. Turn _____ is fair play.
7. Wisdom; education

8. Homophone of "too" and "two"
9. A large swelling wave that breaks on the coast
10. A large flat fish; or a cheap fellow
11. Definite article, as in "_____ early bird gets _____ worm."
12. A hard surface on which people stroll

V. On the left, below, is a sign that carefully tells visitors how to treat (or how *not* to treat) the animals in the San Diego Zoo. (Obviously some employees had fun with a thesaurus!) **A *thesaurus* is a dictionary of synonyms and antonyms, that is, of words with similar meanings and words with opposite meanings.** A thesaurus is a useful tool for any writer. Using your own thesaurus or dictionary, create at the right a sign that would be appropriate in a gift shop specializing in china and glass objects.

**PLEASE DO NOT
ANNOY, TORMENT,
PESTER, PLAGUE,
MOLEST, WORRY,
BADGER, HARRY,
HARASS, HECKLE,
PERSECUTE, IRK,
BULLYRAG, VEX,
DISQUIET, GRATE,
BESET, BOTHER,
TEASE, NETTLE,
TANTALIZE, OR
RUFFLE THE ANIMALS**

VI. As you know, the *vowels* are *a, e, i, o,* and *u*. All the rest of the letters of the alphabet are *consonants*. Here's a new word game that makes good use of vowels and consonants. Example:

Add a consonant to *pate* and get something sticky.   pa S te

1. Add a consonant to *moor* and get something that runs.   _____

2. Add a vowel to *cost* and get a seashore.   _____

3. Add a consonant to *meal* and get an award.   _____

4. Add a vowel to *hose* and get a building.   _____

5. Add a consonant to *root* and get a mechanical person.   _____

VII. If you insert an appropriate preposition in each of the blanks below, the sentences will make sense (though the customer doesn't!). You may use each preposition only *once*.

Danny ran _____ the store _____ the end _____ the street. _____ his pocket he took a dime and placed it _____ the counter. "I want ice cream _____ chocolate syrup, and soda _____ a tall glass," he said. "I want peanuts in a circle _____ the ice cream, and a cherry _____ the top."

The storeowner looked at the dime and chuckled. "Would you settle _____ two peanuts and the cherry?" he asked.

21. BOAT JAMBOREE

Suppose the time is thousands and thousands of years ago. You're looking for a new home, and you have all your belongings in a couple of bundles. And then you come to a wide lake. You look across longingly, but it's too far to swim. So how do you get across?

Well, you might take a bundle of reeds, tie them together, lie on them, and paddle. Or you might find an old log near the bank and use it in the same way. Or you might turn a large empty jar into a tiny raft.

If you were a bit more sophisticated, you might stitch an animal skin, blow it up, and literally float across the water. If you were a good deal more sophisticated, you might bind together several inflated animal skins or several logs to make a raft that would carry you across in comfort.

All these methods of water-transportation actually worked in the pre-boat era. Since then, human inventiveness has created all kinds of boats and ships.

. . . the ARK. Remember Noah's? That early ark was a large vessel, 500 feet long and more than eighty feet wide. Even today, large and bulky ships are often called arks.

. . . the CANOE. This small open boat with pointed ends was first made of skins or bark, later of wood or aluminum. It was popular with American Indians and is still popular today for lake and river traveling.

. . . the FERRY. This boat, large or small, moves across a particular body of water on schedule. It carries people and cars and all kinds of goods.

. . . the SLOOP. This is a single-masted, fore-and-aft rigged sailing vessel, used often for pleasure sailing and for racing.

. . . the PRIVATEER. This is a privately owned ship authorized by a government to capture enemy vessels in wartime. Privateers were active in the Revolutionary and Civil Wars.

. . . the JUNK. This is a Chinese ship, usually flat-bottomed, with a high stern and battened sails.

. . . the YACHT. This is a fairly small sailing or motor-operated vessel used for cruising and racing.

. . . the TUG. This is a small but very powerful boat that tows larger vessels into or out of port.

And this is only the beginning! In addition, there are barges, battleships, tramps and clippers, catamarans and catboats, houseboats, and skiffs, trawlers, liners, yawls, and dinghies, gondolas, frigates, motorboats, and shells . . . and still others.

Select any two of the vessels *not* defined above. Check a dictionary and write the definitions below.

1. _____

_____

2. _____

_____

A NAUTICAL VOCABULARY

You'll be laughed at for being a LANDLUBBER if you don't know at least a few NAUTICAL TERMS!

Don't talk about the *front* or *back* of a ship; do talk about the *bow* or *stern*. Don't move to the *right* or *left;* do move to the *starboard* or *port*. And don't talk about the sail that runs along the center; do talk about the sail that runs *fore-and-aft*.

The *keel* is the backbone of a vessel. It's a long piece of wood or metal that runs from bow to stern and to which the frames are attached. If a boat *keels*, it capsizes, or over-turns. If you keel over, you capsize, or fall down!

An *anchor* is a heavy steel or iron object connected by a cable to a vessel. When thrown overboard, an anchor holds a boat in one position. You can also *anchor* a tent rope to the ground with a stake, or play *anchorman* (or *anchorwoman* or *anchorperson*): the strongest member of a team.

A ship doesn't travel at miles per hour. It travels at *knots*. A knot equals one nautical mile, and one nautical mile equals 1.1508 land miles. Therefore, a ship with a 10-knot speed covers 10 nautical miles (or 11 land miles) in one hour. *Knot* is an interesting word. With or without a dictionary, try to define *knot* as it is used in the following sentences.

1. A *knot* of spectators: _____

2. To tie the *knot:* _____

3. A *knotty* problem: _____

4. A *knot* in a piece of wood: _____

5. A *knot*hole: _____

CURIOUS ABOUT BOATS?

Your curiosity collection is growing. Add a few from the marine world. (Search the library!)

1. What was unusual about the submarine, the *Turtle?*

_____

_____

2. What was unusual about the ship, the *Great Eastern?*

_____

_____

3. What was unusual about the ship, the *Titanic?*

_____

_____

4. What was unusual about the submarine, the *Nautilus?*

_____

_____

ALL ABOARD!

Pull out an *atlas* (a book of maps) and plan a voyage by water. You may sail down a river, cruise along an ocean coast, or head for faraway places! *You* decide. Don't worry about fuel, tides, or even possible speeds. Just plan a three-day voyage that you would like to take.

Example:

Trip from Fort Lauderdale, Florida, to Key West, Florida, along the Atlantic coast

Day One: Head south along the coast to Miami Beach. Land for a few hours. Stroll along the avenues lined with extravagant hotels. Next return to the ship and sail around Biscayne Bay, enjoying the view of lush and beautiful mansions.

Day Two: Head south of Miami Beach and then turn east. Proceed about eight miles toward the Gulf Stream. Anchor. Spend the day trying your hand at deep-sea fishing. At night, return to Miami Beach and dine on your catch.

Day Three: Again head south. Visit a number of the Florida Keys (groups of small islands). Land occasionally for short exploratory trips. Lunch on a Turtle Burger and, for dessert, enjoy Key Lime Pie. Arrive at Key West by late afternoon and visit the Naval Air Station.

It's your turn now. Use strict parallel structure, beginning every sentence with a verb. (Exceptions: preceding the verb, you may sometimes wish to use a transitional word like "next," "then," or "at night." *Transitional words* **link one sentence to another**.) Create a trip you would really like to take!   ⟶

ARKS, BARGES, CATAMARANS, AND DINGHIES

Using any of the nautical names and terms mentioned on pages 138 and 139 (or any others you already know), develop a class nautical dictionary—in rhyme!

Start by turning two of these names or terms into amusing couplets.

Examples:

> The JUNK is a flat-bottomed boat with a sail,
> The Chinese adore the high stern at the tail.   ⟶

> FORE is before, or in front, or ahead,
> AFT is behind, like the last heel of bread.   ⟶

Select the best couplets for each letter of the alphabet, type, add a few amusing line drawings, and mimeograph. Result—a class nautical dictionary guaranteed to make rough seas smooth for even the lowliest landlubber!

ALL ABOARD

Your three-day trip:

_____
_____
_____
_____
_____
_____
_____
_____
_____
_____
_____
_____
_____
_____
_____
_____
_____
_____

ARKS, BARGES, CATAMARANS, AND DINGHIES

_____
_____

_____
_____

A SEA YARN

Sailors love to spin sea yarns—and it's not surprising. Everybody loves stories about ships and storms and the mysterious world at the bottom of the ocean. Have you read

Robert Louis Stevenson's *Treasure Island*, or
Thor Heyerdahl's *Kon-Tiki*, or
Jules Verne's *Twenty Thousand Leagues Under the Sea?*

If you haven't, you should! Meanwhile, you can write your own sea story; but before you begin, you will want to know certain things.

Characters. Have at least two main characters. Describe each briefly, giving age, appearance, and major characteristics. (Make yourself a character, if you like.)

1. _____

_____

2. _____

_____

Destination and Route. Where are your characters going? What route will they follow? Are there any natural problems they will meet (storms, sharks, reefs, rocks, etc.)?

1. Destination: _____

2. Route: _____

3. Natural problems: _____

Other Problems. Perhaps your ship will be attacked by pirates, or will find itself unexpectedly in the middle of a sea battle. Perhaps it will be attacked by helicopters. *You* decide. What other problems will your sailors meet?

_____

_____

Plot. **The *plot* of a story is the action that takes place.** Here is our outline of a plot.

1. A small cabin cruiser leaves Fort Lauderdale for Key West, Florida. It is navigated by sixteen-year-old Michael Forest and his sister, Tammy.
2. They cruise south along the Atlantic coast to Miami Beach. Here they anchor and go ashore for lunch, wishing for a little excitement.
3. Back on board, they head southeast toward an island Tammy has heard of.
4. At first the island seems deserted. They see an old shack. They eavesdrop and hear radio signals and some odd conversation. It's one link in a spy ring!
5. They create a diversion, luring the two men out of the shack. They go in, send a message to the Coast Guard giving their location, then smash the radio equipment. They get back to their boat.
6. The spies have a boat, too. Within minutes Mike and Tammy are being pursued. The enemy boat draws near, and one spy jumps into their boat. There's a three-way fight, and the boat tumbles about in the water.
7. They subdue the one spy, but the second rams his boat into theirs. Then all are tumbling about in the water when—just in the nick of time—the Coast Guard arrives. The spies are captured, and Mike and Tammy return to Fort Lauderdale.

Outline your plot at the top of the facing page.

OUTLINE OF YOUR PLOT

_____

_____

_____

_____

_____

_____

_____

_____

_____

_____

_____

A SEA YARN

Now, of course, you write your story! Remember to use dialogue (see pages 40 and 112) and to create suspense. Your sea yarn may be for children, young people, or adults—as you wish. Begin it below, and continue in your notebook. Good sailing!

_____

_____

_____

_____

_____

_____

_____

_____

_____

_____

_____

_____

22. THE STORY OF BREAD

Bread.

It comes in all shapes: round, cubical, or with a domed top; braided, in the shape of birds and fishes; or tapered like a pyramid.

It is made with different ingredients: with wheat, barley, oats, or millet; with rye or corn. In times of famine it has been made with grass or reeds or the acorns of oaks. It has even been made with pine bark and straw—though this is not recommended.

When it is unleavened, it is flat. When it is leavened (with yeast), it is high and airy. It may be flavored with poppy seeds or sesame, with zucchini or dates or bananas. Or it may be plain.

Whatever it is, it is B-R-E-A-D—the staff of life—the food that has sustained the human race for 10,000 years.

. . . On the walls of one tomb in Egypt are pictures showing the operation of a royal bakery. Two men balance themselves on poles as they *jump* on the dough, kneading it. Others shape it into small loaves. Still others heat the baking dishes. And still others fuel the ovens.

. . . In the ancient world, peasants were sometimes paid in breads. Once, about 3,000 years ago, when some laborers were not given their bread, they decided to "lie down in their homes" and refused to work. This may have been the first strike.

. . . Remember Jason and the Golden Fleece? Some scholars think that Jason was really searching for grain, and that the Golden Fleece was really fields of golden wheat.

. . . In Jerusalem, at the time of Christ, there was a "bakers' street." Here all bakers baked their breads and sold them. Passersby could watch with delight.

. . . In Anglo-Saxon England, the man who owned the soil was called the *hlaford*—meaning the man who gives out the bread. This was later shortened to *lord*. His lady was called the *hlaefdigge*—the kneader of the dough. This was shortened to *lady*.

. . . Bread has always been connected with religion. In ancient Greece the "celebration of the bread" began on September 20 and continued for nine days. Everyone took part in all kinds of religious and social ceremonies.

. . . BREAD SIN occurred when people mishandled bread. In Vineta in the Baltic, some inhabitants closed ratholes with bread. Their punishment: the whole city sank into the sea. In Tyrol, Frau Hitt rubbed her child's clothes with it. Her punishment: she was turned into stone.

"BAKING" BREAD

Do you remember what an anagram is? It's a word made by rearranging the letters of another word. Start rearranging, and find one anagram for BREAD. _____

You can also make three- and four-letter words from the letters in BREAD . . . ERA, for example. Can you find eight more?

_____ _____ _____ _____

_____ _____ _____ _____

A BREAD VOCABULARY

Just as BREAD is part of our daily diet, so it is also part of our daily vocabulary.

All by itself, BREAD can mean several things: the white or rye or wheat loaf, or food in general, or our earnings, or even (slang) money.

A BREADBOARD is simply a piece of wood on which we slice bread.

A BREADWINNER is someone who earns the money to buy the family's food.

A BREAD LINE is a line of people waiting for free food.

A BREADBASKET is usually a geographical region that supplies a great deal of grain for the making of bread; but, as slang, it also refers to a large stomach.

BREAD AND BUTTER is an informal way of referring to the way one makes a living.

A BREAD-AND-BUTTER LETTER is a note thanking someone for hospitality.

TO BREAD meat is to coat meat with bread crumbs before frying it.

TO BREAK BREAD is to eat—even when you're not eating bread.

TO KNOW WHICH SIDE ONE'S BREAD IS BUTTERED ON is to be careful of one's own interests.

And TO TAKE THE BREAD OUT OF SOMEONE'S MOUTH is to take away that person's livelihood.

Select any two of the above words and use each in a sentence *not* about bread.

Word #1: _____

Sentence: _____

Word #2: _____

Sentence: _____

CURIOUS ABOUT BREAD?

Today almost a third of all Americans are baking their own bread. Why? Because we like to see it rise; we like to see the crust turn golden brown; above all, we like to taste it! On page 144 are some curious facts about bread. Turn to several different encyclopedias and to any other reference books you like and find at least three more curious facts about bread. Write them below.

1. _____

_____

2. _____

_____

3. _____

_____

A BREAD PARAPHRASE

Since BREAD is such a popular food, all kinds of BREAD quotations and BREAD proverbs exist, too. One good way to understand a quotation is to *paraphrase* it: **to say it in different words and thereby make it clearer.**

Quotation: "Man cannot live by bread alone." (Bible: Deuteronomy)

Paraphrase: We humans cannot live on just food and material things. We need spiritual food, too. We need to nourish our spirits and our minds as well as our bodies.

Below are seven quotations. Choose four of them and paraphrase each of your choices on the facing page.

1. "Half a loaf is better than none." (Proverb)
2. "Give us this day our daily bread." (Bible: Matthew)
3. "Bread is the staff of life." (Jonathan Swift)
4. "He who has no bread has no authority." (Turkish proverb)
5. "Bread is an army's greatest ally: the soldier marches no farther than his stomach." (Russian proverb)
6. "The first word in a war is spoken by the guns—but the last word has always been spoken by bread." (Herbert Hoover)
7. "Were we directed from Washington when to sow, and when to reap, we should soon want bread." (Thomas Jefferson) ("Want," in this sentence, means "need" or "lack.")

A BREAD-AND-BUTTER LETTER

Any time you spend even one night in someone else's home, you should send your host or hostess a bread-and-butter letter. It may be short, but it should mention a few specific things that you enjoyed during your visit.

August 16, 19___ ___

Dear Uncle Bob,

My weekend visit with you at your camp in the Adirondacks was an unforgettable experience! I loved every minute of it.

I had never fished before, and you were so good about baiting my hook. I'm still bragging about the trout I caught. Weren't they delicious? I'm trying to persuade Mom to fry fish in the backyard in an inground oven!

Thanks again for inviting me. I hope you'll stay with us the next time you are in Philadelphia. I can't take you fishing, but I can introduce you to a couple of fantastic seafood restaurants!

Affectionately,

Jeanne

You try it now. Write a bread-and-butter letter to a friend, relative, or neighbor. Mention one or two things you especially enjoyed. If you make the letter good enough, you may even get a second invitation!

⟶

A BREAD PARAPHRASE

1. _____
   _____
   _____

2. _____
   _____
   _____

3. _____
   _____
   _____

4. _____
   _____
   _____

A BREAD-AND-BUTTER LETTER

                                          _____

_____

_____

_____

_____

_____

_____

_____

_____

_____

_____

_____

                                          _____

A BREAD DOCUMENTARY

Remember the animated cartoon about pigs that you created on page 81? Well, we're going back to TV land again, this time to develop a documentary.

What is a documentary? **A *documentary* is a presentation of facts about someone, something, or some event.** The key word is FACTS. Everything that is presented must be true.

Today television documentaries are popular. They may be about wild animals, or some aspect of the Presidency, or deep-sea diving. One may even be about—BREAD! So your assignment is to plan and describe a documentary about *bread*.

Step 1: Start by selecting a *theme*. Here are two possibilities:

> Bread is the staff of life.
> Bread is the basis of civilization.

You may use one of these or one of your own. What theme do you choose?

_____

Step 2: You already have plenty of material on pages 144 through 147. You also know a good deal about bread from buying it, eating it, and perhaps baking it. List below at least four facts or incidents that will be used as scenes in your documentary.

_____

_____

_____

_____

Step 3: Plan an opening scene. The opening scene, like an introduction to an essay, is vitally important. (If it isn't good, the viewer may switch channels!) You may open with the camera on a field of golden wheat, using color and distance to create interest. Think about it. What scene will you use to open your documentary?

_____

_____

_____

Step 4: Plan a closing scene. The closing scene, like a conclusion to an essay, is also important. It ties things together; it makes a final impact on the viewer. You may wish to close with a series of short shots showing people eating bread in all kinds of situations. What scene will you use to close your documentary?

_____

_____

_____

Step 5: Go back to Step 2. In what order should you present the four major scenes in your documentary? Decide—and number them 1 through 4.

A BREAD DOCUMENTARY

You should be ready now. You have a kind of outline: an introduction, four major scenes, and a conclusion. Go back to page 81 and reread your description of an animated cartoon program. Then, below, read one student's description of a documentary about BREAD. Finally, on separate paper, write a description of your own BREAD documentary. REMEMBER: just *facts*—curious facts about a curious thing.

Introduce the program, its length, and its audience. Give its purpose.	"The Baking of Bread" will be a one-half hour documentary designed for viewers of all ages. It will show how bread has been baked from primitive times to the present.
Describe the opening scene.	The opening scene will show people eating bread: small children in a schoolyard eating sandwiches; a teenager devouring a submarine; women at a bridge party eating tiny decorated sandwiches; construction workers eating thick nutritious sandwiches; a baby munching on a hard crust; a commuter at a counter buttering a roll and eating it. The scene will end with pieces of toast popping wildly out of toasters as Americans settle down for breakfast.
Describe scene #2.	Scene #2 will show primitive peoples grinding corn, mixing it with water, shaping it into thin, round loaves, and baking these loaves on hot rocks. A narrator will point out that this is probably how bread was first baked.
Describe scene #3. (From item on page 144)	Scene #3 will open with a picture of the tomb in Egypt that shows the operation of a royal bakery. Then the scene will "come to life" as actors mix the dough and jump on it, kneading it to the proper consistency. The entire baking procedure in ancient Egypt will be portrayed, step-by-step.
Describe scene #4.	Scene #4 will bring the viewer to this country over 300 years ago. Close-ups will show the early colonists using long-poled shovels to place the bread in chimney ovens. This scene will include the baking of hardtack, or sea bread, popular then because it could be carried by travelers or sailors. It was hard and not very tasty, but it lasted for a long time and was moderately nutritious.
Describe scene #5.	Scene #5 will begin with a series of views of modern bakeries and then go on to explain commercial baking on a large scale. It will cover the entire procedure from the harvesting of wheat to the distribution of bread in giant trucks to supermarkets.
Describe concluding scene.	The concluding scene will show bakers today: home bakers as well as commercial bakers. Coming out of all kinds of ovens will be round, rectangular, and oval loaves, twisted breads, horns, hard rolls and soft, fruit breads, nut breads, etc. The scene will end with a close-up of one beautiful loaf of bread, still visibly hot. Members of a family smile as they approach it with knives and butter.

23. A TALE OF A TUB

What good is a *bathtub*, anyway?

Well, you can use one to wash venetian blinds, or heavy drapes, or an outsized quilt. (People do.)

You can use one to sail toy ships or quacking plastic ducks. (Kids do.)

You can use one as a planter in which to grow flowers and vegetables. (Some immigrants did in the early 20th century in the big cities.)

You can use one as a status symbol—by reclining in it to have your portrait painted. (A few wealthy aristocrats in Victorian England did.)

You can even use it to participate in a "boat" race. Just equip it with an outboard motor and cart it up to Vancouver, British Columbia. A bathtub race takes place there annually. The record: 24 hours to cover 36.6 miles.

You can even use it to take a bath!

... President Andrew Jackson threw the bathtub out of the White House. He said it was undemocratic.

... In ancient Rome small tubs were hung by ropes from the ceiling. In them, one could "rock and roll" while bathing.

... Also in ancient Rome, the Baths of Diocletian, built in 302, could accommodate 3200 people at one time. These huge public baths were social centers, political forums, and gymnasiums ... as well as baths.

... Bathtubs have come in all shapes. In the late 18th century they were made in the shape of chaise longues, with padded backs like sofas, round like chairs. They were once made in the form of a boot. With only the shoulders and head showing, the Boot Bath was both modest and warm.

... In America in 1897 a tub with a lid was advertised. It could double as a bed.

... The French playwright, Edmond Rostand, wrote *Cyrano de Bergerac* in the bathtub. It was the only place where he wasn't disturbed.

... If you used the water going over Niagara Falls to fill the country's bathtubs, you could fill 4,000 every second, or 240,000 every minute. At that rate you could fill the nation's 100 million tubs in just a little over eight hours!

CHANGE A STORY

You can change a pleasant story to a horror story simply by substituting a few antonyms for the words in parentheses. Try it.

The bathtub in my hotel room was (long) _____ and (wide) _____. The water, very (hot) _____, (poured) _____ from the tap. (Quickly) _____ the tub filled. I lowered myself into the (deep) _____ water and (stretched) _____ my legs. It was (marvelous) _____! My skin grew (smooth) _____, my muscles (relaxed) _____. I experienced only (pleasure) _____. This bathtub was indeed my (dream) _____ come true—my passport to (Paradise) _____!

SIMON SAYS . . .

Here's a variation of an old game. Whatever sentence structure Simon uses, *you* use! For content of your sentences, use "bathtub" material on the preceding page. You may use each item on page 150 only once. Example:

Simon Says: Queen Victoria considered bathtubs unnecessary.

You say: **President Andrew Jackson considered bathtubs undemocratic.** _____

1. *Simon Says:* Bathtubs can be used to wash curtain rods and lampshades.

   You say: _____

2. *Simon Says:* A folding bathtub, which can disappear into a closet, saves space.

   You say: _____

3. *Simon Says:* Why were the free public baths in New York City so popular?

   You say: _____

4. *Simon Says:* Wealthy Victorians sat in their bathtubs while receiving honored guests.

   You say: _____

5. *Simon Says:* Bathtubs are occasionally used as planters!

   You say: _____

6. *Simon Says:* Benjamin Franklin, the American statesman, liked to read in the bathtub.

   You say: _____

WHAT'S THE QUESTION?

Below are some answers. All you have to do is provide the questions. Example:

Question: **When did American hotels first provide bathtubs?** _____

Answer: American hotels first provided bathtubs after the Civil War.

1. *Question:* _____

   Answer: Queen Elizabeth I of England bathed once a month whether she needed it or not.

2. *Question:* _____

   Answer: The French nobles in the 18th century sometimes had two bathtubs so they could wash in one and rinse in the other.

3. *Question:* _____

   Answer: More people are drowned in bathtubs than are killed by sharks.

4. *Question:* _____

   Answer: A shower uses only about half the water that a tub bath does.

5. *Question:* _____

   Answer: More than 150,000 injuries a year occur in bathtubs and showers, and almost half of these require emergency treatment.

MORE OF "SIMON SAYS"—BUT WITH A DIFFERENCE!

SIMON SAYS: *revision* is one key to good writing. It can turn a dull paragraph into a fascinating one! As you revise, you will want to combine sentences, add illustrations, and rearrange ideas, all for two purposes: to make your meaning more clear, and to catch and hold your reader's attention.

Below is a paragraph that is written correctly, but it is dull. Read it. Then follow Simon's instructions and rewrite it on the facing page.

[1]A bathtub is versatile. [2]It can be used as a planter. [3]It can also be used as a status symbol. [4]It can be used to sail boats. [5]It can be used to sail plastic ducks. [6]It can be used to read in or to write in. [7]It can even be used as a boat. [8]It can be used to wash drapes and quilts. [9]It can be used to wash lampshades.

SIMON SAYS:

Keep the first sentence as is.

Combine sentences 2 and 3. Do this by eliminating the words "It can also be used" in sentence 3. Add "and" after "planter."

Combine sentences 4 and 5 in the same way.

Add illustrations in sentence 6. After "read in," add one illustration in parentheses; for example, (Benjamin Franklin did!). After "write in," add another illustration in parentheses. Find one on page 150.

Save sentence 7 for the last sentence. It's the most dramatic.

Combine sentences 8 and 9 by using "drapes, quilts, and lampshades" as a series.

Now use sentence 7 as your concluding sentence. Punctuate with an exclamation point.

When you have finished, read the original paragraph, and then read your revised paragraph. Doesn't revision make a difference?

SIMON SAYS: Now read the following paragraph.

Bathtubs come in all shapes and sizes. Some are very small. These are for babies. Some are very large. These can hold as many as twenty people at one time. Some look like slippers. Some look like boots. Some look like sofas. Some look like chairs. Some are hung by ropes from the ceiling. You can "rock and roll" in these while bathing. Some have lids. These can serve as beds. Some look like bags.

SIMON SAYS: Revise this in any way you like!

You may—combine sentences,
—change the order of sentences,
—add words,
—delete words, or
—change punctuation.

SIMON SAYS: Good luck!

MORE OF "SIMON SAYS"—BUT WITH A DIFFERENCE!

Your revision of paragraph 1:

_____
_____
_____
_____
_____
_____
_____
_____
_____
_____

Your revision of paragraph 2:

_____
_____
_____
_____
_____
_____
_____
_____
_____
_____
_____
_____
_____
_____
_____
_____
_____

YOUR TALE OF A TUB

Just about everyone has had an amusing experience in a tub. Perhaps you dropped a math book into the tub while bathing; perhaps you bathed a baby who loved to splash; perhaps you were in a tub when the lights went out. If you haven't had an interesting experience in a bathtub, make one up. Then describe it below.

_____

_____

_____

_____

_____

_____

_____

_____

_____

Good. Now revise it on the facing page. Do you have

. . . a good reader-catching first sentence?

. . . different types of sentences (declarative, interrogative, imperative, and exclamatory)?

. . . different types of sentence structure (simple, compound, complex)?

. . . some long sentences and some short?

. . . a little humor?

. . . a dramatic last sentence?

Make any changes that will improve your paragraph, and write the revised paragraph on the facing page. Read both. If the revised paragraph is better, more interesting than the original, you're progressing well with your writing!

A BATHTUB LIMERICK

A *limerick* **is a humorous five-line poem. The 1st, 2nd, and 5th lines are fairly long, and they rhyme. The 3rd and 4th lines are shorter, and** *they* **rhyme.**
Here is an example of a bathtub limerick:

> There once was a lady named Pinner   (a)
> Who grew thinner and thinner and thinner;   (a)
>   Till she stepped in the tub   (b)
>   And started to rub   (b)
> And erased herself just before dinner!   (a)

Read the limerick several times to get the "feel" of it. Then dream up an amusing situation with a bathtub and start writing on the facing page. Your first line should begin . . .

     There once was a _____

Have fun!

YOUR TALE OF A TUB

Your revision:

_____
_____
_____
_____
_____
_____
_____
_____
_____
_____
_____
_____
_____
_____
_____
_____
_____
_____
_____
_____

A BATHTUB LIMERICK

_____
_____
_____
_____
_____

24. PET PEEVES

It isn't the big problems that drive us mad—that cause family squabbles and broken friendships. It's the pet peeves—the little things—that infuriate us.

It's late at night; you're starved; and you think of the strawberry shortcake that was left from dinner. Ah, yes! There's the yellow plastic container it was in. You grab it eagerly. You open it. It's empty. You are peeved.

Then there's the person who opens closet and cabinet doors and *never* shuts them.

There is the dentist who fills your mouth with all sorts of equipment and then asks you a question.

There is your mother who, after you've paid $10 for a styling job, says seriously: "I thought you were going to get a haircut."

There's the soupy soap left after a shower, and there's the bottle of shampoo minus its cap.

There's the phone number, all by itself (to whom does it belong?).

There's the person who dreamed about you and got mad because of what you did in the dream.

And there's the forever uncertain soul who, when asked: "What do you want to eat? What movie would you like to see? What television program would you like to watch?" answers: "I don't care. It doesn't make any difference!"

Yes. Little things mean a lot. It's the little things we can't handle; and that's not surprising, for they often occur daily. Imagine—if you leave soupy soap in the soap dish every day, that's 365 times a year, 3,650 times in ten years, 7,300 times in twenty years! (No wonder parents become irritable!)

A PEEVE POLL

Begin your probe into pet peeves by taking a poll. (If possible, poll people in a group. One answer often triggers three others.) Simply ask: "What is your pet peeve?" List below the results of your poll.

_____

_____

_____

_____

_____

_____

_____

_____

_____

_____

A PEEVE VOCABULARY

"Peeve" words are unpleasant; still, you should know a few.

infuriated—maddened; made very angry

trivial—of little importance; minor; petty

inconsequential—too unimportant to have consequences or results; petty

source of friction—source (beginning point) + friction (conflict or disagreement); therefore, source of friction = beginning point of a conflict or disagreement

exasperated—very irritated; about out of patience

sullen—sulky; in a bad mood

vexed—irritated; annoyed; bothered

wrathful—full of violent anger

Select any two of the above. Use each of the two in a sentence about pet peeves.

Word #1: _____

Sentence: _____

_____

Word #2: _____

Sentence: _____

_____

A PEEVE PROBE

Why are we "peeved" by pet peeves? A little thinking gives the answer. When the dentist fills our mouths with equipment and then asks a question, we're peeved because he's asking the impossible. We want to answer and can't! When we find an empty container in the refrigerator, we're peeved because we're disappointed. We were all ready to eat something good, had it in our hands (we thought), and then discovered—nothing!

Choose three of the pet peeves you listed on page 156, as a result of your poll. In each case explain in a sentence or two why it is likely to peeve someone.

1. the peeve: _____

the explanation: _____

_____

2. the peeve: _____

the explanation: _____

_____

3. the peeve: _____

the explanation: _____

_____

AN ANECDOTE, AND THEN . . .

Pet peeves can easily be turned into anecdotes. After all, they're short, they concern human nature, and they're usually at least mildly interesting.

Choose one of the pet peeves you listed on page 156 and write a short anecdote about it, on the facing page. First read this example written by one student. ⟶

> One of my pet peeves is people who borrow ballpoint pens and then walk off with them. A friend of mine does this all the time. She never has a pen of her own, and so she borrows mine. She must have borrowed hundreds of pens from me in the last five years. I don't mind too much—they're not very expensive. But I do mind always finding myself without a pen when I always start off with one!

> As a school assignment, that isn't bad . . . just a little flat, like soda that's been standing in an uncapped bottle for a week. But if you were planning to use it as part of an article in a newspaper, it wouldn't do at all. Let's take the same anecdote and see what can be done with it.

Here are some possibilities for revision:

1. Change first-person "I" to third-person, "he" or "she."
2. Sharpen the first sentence, dramatizing the pet peeve.
3. Give most of the information as quotes.
4. Use an *exact* statistic rather than a general number.
5. Use a little alliteration or a simile.
6. End with a quote, one with an unexpected twist.

AN ANECDOTE AGAIN!

Here is the same anecdote, rewritten, following the above suggestions:

Stronger beginning: "ball-point pen stealers."

Ballpoint-pen stealers are a major source of friction for many people. They're not real thieves—just borrowers who forget to return.

Quotes.
Alliteration: "pen-pincher."

"My friend Lee is an incurable pen-pincher," said one student at Merrydale High School who has learned to buy pens wholesale. "Lee can buy five pens on Monday and lose them all by Monday night. Tuesday she's back to borrowing mine—and then walking off with it.

Quotes continued.
Rhetorical question.
Exact statistic.
Appalling realization.

"That leaves *me* without a pen in most of my classes. Can't you just see teachers believing this story? I figure Lee has borrowed 614 pens from me in the last five years. Come to think of it—at 19¢ apiece, that's $116.66!"

Interruption, followed by continuation of quote.
Conclusion.

She paused, her eyes suddenly cold. "I think," she said, pronouncing each word crisply, "it's time I found myself a less expensive friend!"

Isn't that a much better anecdote? Rewrite yours now, on the facing page. ⟶

AN ANECDOTE, AND THEN . . .

Anecdote about your pet peeve:

_____

_____

_____

_____

_____

_____

_____

_____

_____

AN ANECDOTE AGAIN!

Your anecdote revised:

_____

_____

_____

_____

_____

_____

_____

_____

_____

_____

_____

_____

_____

_____

_____

PACKAGING PEEVES

The editor of your local newspaper has asked you to write an article about PEEVES. (OK—this is far-fetched; but so was the moon-landing!) You agree.

1. The first job of any writer is to find an *angle*. You've already done your preparatory work: you've listed pet peeves; you've thought about them; you've considered their effect on others. You've even written an anecdote about one of them.

   To find an *angle*, ask yourself questions like these:

   Do I want to write about pet peeves in general—a sort of wandering essay?
   Or do I want to write, in detail, about one pet peeve?
   Do I want to write about pet peeves today compared to pet peeves of the past? (If I choose this, I'll have to talk to some older people for additional information.)
   Do I want to concentrate on pet peeves that exist in husband-wife relationships, *or* in parent-child relationships, *or* in teacher-student relationships?
   Do I want to write about the effects of pet peeves: divorces, broken friendships, even occasional violence?

   Think hard. Then decide what your angle will be and write it below.

   _____

   _____

2. Ask yourself: do I need any additional information? If you do, list below the *kinds* of information you need: for example, statistics, pet peeves of the past, quotations, etc.

   _____

   Now get this information and make notes on a piece of scrap paper.

3. Organize your material by making an informal outline on scrap paper. (See pages 142 and 148.)

4. Write your feature article about PET PEEVES on scrap paper. Remember the six suggestions for writing a good anecdote on page 158. Use some or all of them, as you wish. But write sharply—with color—with details—with quotations!

   After you have finished writing your article, return to step #5 below.

5. Write "yes" or "no" after each of the following questions:

   a. Is your introductory paragraph interesting, forceful, or appealing? _____

   b. Are your sentences varied? Some long and some short? _____ Some simple, some compound, some complex? _____ One or two questions? _____

   c. Did you use a couple of quotations? _____ A bit of alliteration? _____ A simile? _____ A touch of humor? _____

   d. Is your conclusion either unexpected or forceful or dramatic? _____

Look at your answers. Then revise your article accordingly. Write the completed (and polished) article on the facing page. It should be a piece of writing you can be proud of, one you would like to see printed in the newspaper under *your* name! Is it?

PACKAGING PEEVES

Your feature article about Pet Peeves:

_____

_____

_____

_____

_____

_____

_____

_____

_____

_____

_____

_____

_____

_____

_____

_____

_____

_____

_____

_____

_____

_____

_____

_____

_____

25. SUN POWER!

*Each morning, in the east, a brilliant golden ball rises above
the horizon. All day it wheels majestically across the sky.
In late afternoon or early evening, it disappears into the west—
and darkness blankets our land.*

OUR SUN. Without it, we could not survive. Without it, no other living thing could survive. Even the earliest human beings watched it with wonder and fear.

OUR SUN: giver of heat and light; giver of dreams; giver of life itself.

1 . . . The sun is 93 million miles from earth. If we could travel at the speed of light, we could arrive there in eight minutes and ten seconds—but we would be burned to a crisp.

2 . . . In different times and in different countries, the sun has been called a mirror, a jaguar, a monster, and a nocturnal giant.

3 . . . Without the sun, there would be no wind.

4 . . . According to Greek mythology, the sun-god Helios each day drove his golden chariot from his palace in the east to his second palace in the west. One day he permitted his son, Phaethon, to drive the chariot. Phaethon couldn't control the horses. The boy plunged to the ground, and where he landed, the ground was scorched. And so part of the Sahara, the largest desert in the world, was created.

5 . . . The sun is huge. You could place more than a million earths inside the sun without overcrowding.

6 . . . The sun's rays, focused with a magnifying glass, can cause fire. Twenty-three centuries ago the Greek, Archimedes, used mirrors to focus the sun's rays on the wooden ships of the Romans. They burned.

7 . . . Solar energy heats some houses today and may heat all of them in the future.

8 . . . In 1953, UNESCO developed a "solar kitchen" for use in underdeveloped countries. It is a mirror focused on a pot of water. Within fifteen minutes the sun's rays will bring the water to a boil.

9 . . . The sun probably has only five to ten billion more years of life.

SUN POWER

Even the two words, SUN POWER, are powerful! From them, you can create many things. You can create a human feature: N O S E. You can create a church bench: P E W. *You* complete the following creations, using the letters in the words SUN POWER.

1. You can create someone to take care of you when you are ill: _ _ _ _ _ _.

2. You can create hot liquid nourishment: _ _ _ _ _.

3. You can create crystallized water that is fun to play in: _ _ _ _ _.

4. You can create a dried plum: _ _ _ _ _ _.

5. You can create a male descendent: _ _ _ _.

6. You can create a noise made while sleeping: _ _ _ _ _ _.

A SUN VOCABULARY

The SUN is so powerful that you can build a sun vocabulary and increase your defining skills at the same time—just by answering the questions below. You *may* use a dictionary; you *must* use complete sentences!

    Example: Why is a *sunburn* called a SUNburn?

        A sunburn is called a SUNburn because it is the burning or blistering of the skin from too much exposure to the direct rays of the sun.

1. Why is *Sunday* called SUNday? _____

_____

2. Why is a *sun deck* called a SUN deck? _____

_____

3. Why are certain fried eggs called SUNny-side up? _____

_____

4. Why is a *sunstroke* called a SUNstroke? _____

_____

CURIOUS ABOUT THE SUN?

One way to satisfy your curiosity about any subject is to develop a bibliography. A *bibliography* is a list of books, magazine articles, and newspaper articles about a particular subject.

How do you go about developing a bibliography about the SUN? It's fairly easy. Go to the library and check (under SUN and under SOLAR) . . .

        the card catalog,
        several encyclopedias, and
        the *Readers' Guide to Periodical Literature.*

Then list below at least eight books or articles about the SUN and its power. For books, give author, title, publishing company, and date of publication. For articles, give author, title, name of magazine or newspaper, and date of magazine or newspaper.

_____

_____

_____

_____

_____

_____

_____

Now—to satisfy your curiosity about the SUN, all you have to do is consult one or more of the items in your bibliography! Efficient, isn't it?

SUN ACTION

Put to work your Roget's *Thesaurus* (or any other dictionary of synonyms) to find some good action verbs to describe the sun's journey across the sky.

Below are four descriptions of the sun's movements, each ending with a sentence in which the verb is italicized. Find two good synonyms for each of the italicized words and place them in the appropriate blanks on the facing page.

1. The Egyptians believed that each day the sun god got into a boat and was rowed across the sky. One could say that the sun *sailed* across the sky.

2. Some early peoples believed that the sun god had wings. One could say that the sun *flew* across the sky.

3. Some ancient Greeks believed that the sun god drove a golden chariot across the sky. One could say that the sun *rolled* across the sky.

4. In our time, we can be more free. We can say that the sun *ploughed* its way across the sky, or *patrolled* the sky, or *skated* across the sky. This time find two good action verbs—not necessarily synonyms—that would be appropriate to describe the sun's movement.

SUN REVISION

Here is a brief exercise in revision that should increase your writing power. Work on the facing page.

1. Turn item 7 (on page 162) into one question and one answer.

2. In item 8, there are *seven* prepositional phrases. (See page 130.) Find them and list them. Read the sentences without them. Are prepositional phrases essential to the meaning of a sentence?

3. Combine the second and third sentences of item 4 into one compound sentence . . . that is, two sentences connected by the conjunction *and*, *but*, or *or*.

4. Combine the two sentences of item 5 into one complex sentence beginning with the subordinate conjunction *because*.

5. In item 3, the prepositional phrase can be placed at the end of the sentence rather than at the beginning. If you were writing about the importance of the SUN, however, it would be better to keep it where it is—at the beginning. Why?

6. Rewrite item 2 as four short simple sentences. Then read the original sentence and the revised sentences. Which would usually be preferable? Why?

SUN ACTION

1. *a.* The sun _____ across the sky.

   b. The sun _____ across the sky.

2. *a.* The sun _____ across the sky.

   b. The sun _____ across the sky.

3. *a.* The sun _____ across the sky.

   b. The sun _____ across the sky.

4. *a.* The sun _____ across the sky.

   b. The sun _____ across the sky.

SUN REVISION

1. _____

   _____

   _____

2. _____

   _____

   _____

3. _____

   _____

   _____

4. _____

   _____

5. _____

   _____

6. _____

   _____

   _____

   _____

   _____

A PARAGRAPH PARADE

Strike up the drums—and set up your own personal parade of paragraphs!

First comes the music! Every parade begins with a band to stir up the blood of the spectators. Make your first paragraph a "hymn to the sun"—an excited, fast-moving description of a day in the life of the sun. Remember the fine action verbs you collected on p. 164.

> That August morning, the sun rose furiously. Instead of peeping shyly above the horizon, it leapt high, casting hot golden beams on a stunned world. All day long it played in the sky, racing, spinning, doing crazy cartwheels. And all day long the temperature stayed above 100°. At day's end, a still-glowing red, it sank slowly into the west, reluctant to leave. The temperature fell a degree or two. And as we fought for breath, we paid quiet honor to the power and the glory of the sun.

Your turn. Describe the sun on one memorable day. Use action verbs. Make it truly a "hymn to the sun." →

Next come the marching columns! Every parade has marchers, moving along in crisp, parallel lines. Make your second paragraph a group of parallel sentences, moving just as crisply.

> Our sun is the source of life. With it, we can grow fields of golden wheat and acres of green vegetables. With it, we can nourish fruitful orchards, yielding apples and pears, plums and oranges. With its light, we can see. With its heat, we can keep our blood warm and circulating. With it, we are—A-L-I-V-E.

Your turn. Select any topic related to the sun. Write a topic sentence like the first one above. Follow with four or five parallel sentences, each beginning with the same phrase. →

Finally come the fantastic floats! Every parade has floats—and the more there are, the merrier! For crowds love them. With a little imagination and some logic, you can develop a verbal float: a dramatic scene related to the sun.

> It's a dark and dreary world. A few people, wrapped in fur skins, huddle together, shivering in the cold. They live in a cave surrounded by rocks. There are few trees and bushes and no flowers. Their faces are sad, their movements slow and clumsy. Then suddenly the SUN appears! It soars across the heavens, its golden wings wakening a light breeze, its fire sending off waves of heat and glorious light. Green grass softens the earth; and trees, plants, and bright-hued flowers come forth. With the trees, the people build comfortable homes. From the plants, they create delicious foods. Their faces light up with joy. They dance, leap high, and sing long happy songs. All has changed—with the coming of the SUN!

Your turn. Make a verbal float, using any dramatic sun-related scene. Build the color, the suspense. Make it seem visible! →

A PARAGRAPH PARADE

Paragraph #1: A description of the sun.

_____
_____
_____
_____
_____
_____
_____

Paragraph #2: Crisp parallel sentences.

_____
_____
_____
_____
_____
_____
_____
_____

Paragraph #3: A verbal "float."

_____
_____
_____
_____
_____
_____
_____
_____
_____
_____
_____

TIME-OUT—V

I. Play detective! If you don't, you will miss a great deal of life. For detection is observation + the drawing of conclusions. Sherlock Holmes could do it. Do you think you can?

Below is an advertisement for a Turkish Bath Establishment in New York City in the 19th century.* Study it carefully. Then, on the right, write a few paragraphs describing what you can learn about the 19th century just by studying this advertisement. Some things to include: architecture, costumes, methods of transportation, social customs. See how much *you* can deduce!

NEW YORK HYGIENIC HOTEL,

TURKISH BATHS

AND TURKISH BATH ESTABLISHMENT.

Nos 13 & 15 LAIGHT ST.   NEW YORK,
OPPOSITE 395 CANAL ST.

BATHING HOURS

6 to 8 A.M. & 1 to 9 P.M.   GENTS: Sundays 6 to 12 A.M.

LADIES: 10 to 12 A.M.

_____

_____

_____

_____

_____

_____

_____

_____

_____

_____

_____

_____

_____

_____

_____

_____

_____

_____

When you have finished, compare results. If you made *all* the observations and drew *all* the conclusions—congratulations, Sherlock!

---

*From EGGPLANTS, ELEVATORS, ETC. by James Meyers, copyright 1978 Hart Publishing Company, Inc.

II. Remember homophones? (See page 20.) Because they sound alike but have different spellings and meanings, you can use them in a hilarious party game. Just give your guests a list of homophones and challenge them to use one or two in a silly couplet. Here's one example.

> He let out a BAWL although he was tall—
> He had no date for the Mardi Gras BALL!

Notice that the first homophone is in the middle of the first line and rhymes with the last word of the first line. The second homophone is at the end of the second line and rhymes with the last word of the first line.

Here's another.

> In a HANGAR lived Betty Sanger.
> She kept six coats on one coat HANGER.

Here are a few pairs of homophones. Select two pairs and use each pair in a silly couplet.

dye—die	soar—sore	core—corps	fakir—faker
ark—arc	sun—son	bread—bred	idle—idol
duel—dual	knot—not	carat—carrot	break—brake

_____

_____

_____

_____

III. Here's another icebreaker: a stunt that will break the ice, or warm up a party. Just give each guest an unusual plant name. Ask each person to write a paragraph describing the way that plant probably looks. Later ask each person to read the paragraph aloud as you hold up a picture of how the plant really looks.

Here are some unusual plant names that you can use.

Horsetail	Monkey puzzle tree	Bouncing bet
Turtlehead	Petticoat narcissus	Joshua tree
Fiddlehead	Dutchman's breeches	Old man's beard

Try one. Choose one of the above names and write a paragraph describing it . . . as you _imagine_ it might look.

_____

_____

_____

_____

_____

Now compare it to the way the plant _really_ looks. See page 190. How good an imagination do you have?

Words in Review

IV. Continue playing detective. See if you can track down in the diagram below twenty-six of the words used in this text. You may move from left to right, or from top to bottom. Just circle each word as you find it. Next to the diagram, as clues, are definitions. The number of blanks after each definition indicates the number of letters in the word you are looking for. Write the words on the appropriate blanks.

D	L	I	M	E	R	I	C	K	A	S	P
O	V	Q	A	N	A	G	R	A	M	Y	A
C	O	U	P	L	E	T	C	L	O	N	R
U	W	A	S	I	D	I	O	M	R	O	A
M	E	T	I	F	P	N	N	M	A	N	P
E	L	R	M	S	U	B	S	I	L	Y	H
N	E	A	I	A	N	T	O	N	Y	M	R
T	A	I	L	R	T	A	N	I	E	D	A
A	R	N	E	K	O	F	A	B	L	E	S
R	E	V	I	S	I	O	N	R	A	N	E
Y	A	N	E	C	D	O	T	E	L	E	D
B	I	B	L	I	O	G	R	A	P	H	Y

1. A list of books or articles about a particular subject _ _ _ _ _ _ _ _ _ _ _ _

2. A television program that presents facts about one subject

   _ _ _ _ _ _ _ _ _ _

3. A homophone of "arc" _ _ _ _

4. A two-line poem that rhymes

   _ _ _ _ _ _ _

5. A word formed by rearranging the letters of another word _ _ _ _ _ _ _

6. The lesson taught by a fable _ _ _ _ _ _

7. A prefix meaning "little" _ _ _ _ _

8. A brief story that teaches a lesson _ _ _ _ _ _

9. A prefix meaning "far off" _ _ _ _ _

10. A preposition: *The Stories _ _ Mother Goose*

11. Act of rewriting; making corrections, changing words in writing _ _ _ _ _ _ _ _

12. To rewrite something in different words _ _ _ _ _ _ _ _ _ _

13. A four-line poem or stanza _ _ _ _ _ _ _ _

14. The contents of an atlas _ _ _ _ _

15. A comparison using "like" or "as" _ _ _ _ _ _ _

16. Any of the letters "a, e, i, o, u" _ _ _ _ _ _

17. Any letter *not* "a, e, i, o, u" _ _ _ _ _ _ _ _ _

18. A word that means the same as another word _ _ _ _ _ _ _

19. A play on words _ _ _

20. A brief, often humorous story _ _ _ _ _ _ _ _ _

21. A five-line poem—rhyme scheme: a, a, b, b, a _ _ _ _ _ _ _ _

22. A prefix meaning "under" _ _ _ _

23. A word that means the opposite of another word _ _ _ _ _ _ _ _

24. A conjunction: _ _ I were a millionaire, I would buy a yacht.

25. A metal often used in the making of cans _ _ _ _

26. A homophone of "tale" _ _ _ _ _

V. It's time for another COLLYWOBBLE! For directions, see page 136. Ready? Find this riddle—and then solve it! But first you should know that an *idiom* is an expression **with a special meaning not clear from the usual meaning of the words in the expression.** For example, being *on pins and needles* has nothing to do with pins and needles; it is an idiom meaning to be in a state of anxiety, to worry. OK? Now start.

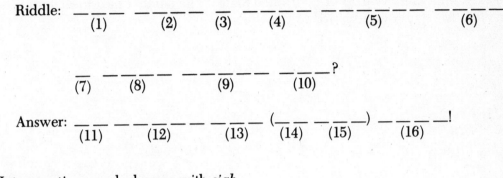

Riddle: _ _ _   _ _ _ _   _ _ _   _ _ _ _   _ _ _ _ _ _   _ _ _ _
       (1)   (2)   (3)   (4)   (5)   (6)

       _ _   _ _ _   _ _ _ _   _ _ _ ?
       (7)   (8)   (9)   (10)

Answer: _ _ _   _ _ _ _ _   _ _ _ _ _ (_ _ _ _ _) _ _ _ _ !
        (11)   (12)   (13)   (14) (15)   (16)

1. Interrogative word; rhymes with *sigh*
2. I do; you do; he, she, or it _____
3. First letter of the alphabet
4. Chief cook in a restaurant; rhymes with the sixth letter of the alphabet
5. Adverb meaning "constantly"
6. Homophone of "ware"
7. Highest grade on a test
8. The missing word in these idioms: _____ and low; _____ and dry; _____ and mighty
9. Antonym of "black"
10. The missing word in these idioms: at the drop of a _____; to pass the _____; talking through one's _____
11. Homophone of "two" and "too"
12. Something placed on something else, usually to protect it
13. Masculine pronoun, possessive case
14. A conjunction that combines two sentences into one compound sentence
15. Feminine pronoun, possessive case
16. The seat of intelligence

VI. You can put together a quick (and varied) dinner just by changing the position of *one* letter in each of the following words.

   For example: Eric (after making "e" the fourth letter) becomes RICE.
               slat (after making "l" the third letter) becomes SALT.

Can you find all ten foods?

barely	⟶ _____	vale	⟶ _____
beard	⟶ _____	gaper	⟶ _____
mate	⟶ _____	stake	⟶ _____
eat	⟶ _____	calm	⟶ _____
Amy	⟶ _____	laws	⟶ _____

THE GRAND FINALE:
The Fabulous Fifty!

One of the most curious of all curious things is that in this country *"fifty equals one"*! We are made up of fifty sovereign states, each fiercely proud of its history, resources, and accomplishments; yet all fifty are even more fiercely proud of being part of the United States of America. That's unique—and worth a little investigation.

Begin by studying this map of the United States. The number next to each state name is the date that state was admitted to the Union.

READING A MAP

Reading a map can be challenging—if you do more than look at it. Study it; make observations; draw conclusions. See how many of the following questions you can answer just by referring to the map of the United States. Answer in complete sentences.

1. Which state touches eight other states? _____

_____

2. In what part of the country are the smallest states found? Can you suggest a reason for this? _____

_____

3. In what part of the country are the largest states found? Can you suggest a reason for this? _____

_____

_____

4. Which states border the Great Lakes and therefore can expect an abundance of snow every winter? _____

_____

5. Desert land in this country is primarily in our Southwest. Which states do you think include large areas of desert land? _____

_____

6. What advantage commercially do states like New York, Virginia, California, and Oregon have over states like Kansas and Nebraska? _____

_____

_____

7. One reads about the "heartland" of this country. Considering what you know about the meaning of "heart," name two or three states that are probably in the "heartland."

_____

8. Which two states are *not* "mainland states"? _____

9. Would you expect there to be more people per square mile in the eastern half of the country, or the western? Why? _____

_____

_____

10. Look closely at the Mississippi and its location. Then try to figure out three ways in which the Mississippi has influenced or affected the states near it. (Do this just by looking at the map and *thinking*.) _____

_____

_____

READING A CHART

On this page and the next three pages is a chart giving information about the fifty states. Check your own state, and glance at the rest. Then skip to page 178.

State	Origin or Meaning of Name	Nickname	Area in sq. miles	Capital
Alabama	Indian: "I clear the thicket."	Cotton State	51,609	Montgomery
Alaska	Eskimo: "Great country"	The Last Frontier	589,757	Juneau
Arizona	Indian: "Place of the little springs"	Sunset State	113,909	Phoenix
Arkansas	Name of Indian tribe	Land of Opportunity	53,104	Little Rock
California	From an imaginary island in a 16th century Spanish romance	Golden State	158,693	Sacramento
Colorado	Spanish: "red," "ruddy"	Silver State	104,247	Denver
Connecticut	Indian: "Beside the long tidal river"	Nutmeg State	5,009	Hartford
Delaware	Name of colonial governor, Lord de la Warr	First State	2,057	Dover
Florida	Spanish: "Abounding in flowers"	Sunshine State	58,560	Tallahassee
Georgia	Name of English king, George II	Peach State	58,876	Atlanta
Hawaii	Not known	Aloha State	6,450	Honolulu
Idaho	Indian: "The sun is coming down the mountain"	Gem State	83,557	Boise
Illinois	Indian: "Tribe of superior men"	Prairie State	56,400	Springfield
Indiana	"Land of Indians"	Hoosier State	36,291	Indianapolis
Iowa	Indian: "This is the place"	Hawkeye State	56,290	Des Moines
Kansas	Indian: "People of the south wind"	Sunflower State	82,264	Topeka
Kentucky	Indian: "Land of tomorrow"	Bluegrass State	40,395	Frankfort
Louisiana	Name of French king, Louis XIV	Pelican State	48,523	Baton Rouge
Maine	French province of Mayne (means "great")	Pine Tree State	33,215	Augusta
Maryland	Name of wife of Charles I of England	Free State	10,577	Annapolis
Massachusetts	Indian: "Big hills"	Bay State	8,257	Boston
Michigan	Indian: "Great lake"	Wolverine State	58,216	Lansing
Minnesota	Indian: "Sky-tinted water"	Gopher State	84,068	St. Paul

Population	Motto	Bird	Flower	Tree
3,742,000	"We dare defend our rights."	yellowhammer	camellia	Southern pine
403,000	"North to the future."	willow ptarmigan	forget-me-not	Sitka spruce
2,354,000	"God enriches."	cactus wren	saguaro cactus	paloverde
2,186,000	"The people rule."	mockingbird	apple blossom	pine
22,294,000	"Eureka." ("I have found it.")	Cal. quail	golden poppy	Cal. redwood
2,670,000	"Nothing without Providence."	lark bunting	columbine	blue spruce
3,099,000	"He who transplanted still sustains."	robin	mountain laurel	white oak
583,000	"Liberty and independence."	blue hen chicken	peach blossom	American holly
8,594,000	"In God we trust."	mockingbird	orange blossom	Sabal palm
5,084,000	"Wisdom, justice, and moderation."	brown thrasher	Cherokee rose	live oak
898,000	"The life of the land is preserved by righteousness."	Hawaiian goose	hibiscus	candlenut
878,000	"May you last forever."	mountain bluebird	syringa	white pine
11,248,000	"State sovereignty, national union."	cardinal	violet	white oak
5,374,000	"The Crossroads of America."	cardinal	peony	tulip poplar
2,896,000	"Our liberties we prize and our rights we will maintain."	eastern goldfinch	wild rose	oak
2,348,000	"To the stars through difficulties."	western meadowlark	sunflower	cottonwood
3,498,000	"United we stand, divided we fall."	cardinal	goldenrod	Kentucky coffee tree
3,966,000	"Union, justice, and confidence."	brown pelican	magnolia	cypress
1,091,000	"I guide."	chickadee	white pine cone & tassel	white pine
4,143,000	"Manly deeds, womanly words."	Baltimore oriole	black-eyed susan	white oak
5,774,000	"By the sword we seek peace, but peace only under liberty."	chickadee	mayflower	American elm
9,189,000	"If you seek a pleasant peninsula, look about you."	robin	apple blossom	white pine
4,008,000	"The North Star."	common loon	pink & white lady's slipper	red pine

State	Origin or Meaning of Name	Nickname	Area in sq. miles	Capital
Mississippi	Indian: "Father of waters"	Magnolia State	47,716	Jackson
Missouri	Indian: "People of the big canoes"	Show Me State	69,686	Jefferson City
Montana	Latin: "Mountainous region"	Treasure State	147,138	Helena
Nebraska	Indian: "River in the flatness"	Cornhusker State	77,227	Lincoln
Nevada	Spanish: "Snow-clad"	Sagebrush State	110,540	Carson City
New Hampshire	County in England	Granite State	9,304	Concord
New Jersey	Name of one of Channel Islands, Jersey	Garden State	7,836	Trenton
New Mexico	From country of Mexico	Land of Enchantment	121,666	Santa Fe
New York	From the Duke of York	Empire State	49,576	Albany
North Carolina	English king, Charles I	Tar Heel State	52,586	Raleigh
North Dakota	Indian tribe, Dakotas	Sioux State	70,665	Bismarck
Ohio	Indian: "Beautiful river"	Buckeye State	41,222	Columbus
Oklahoma	Indian: "Red people"	Sooner State	69,919	Oklahoma City
Oregon	Spanish: "Big-eared men"	Beaver State	96,981	Salem
Pennsylvania	After William Penn's father	Keystone State	45,333	Harrisburg
Rhode Island	Greek island of Rhodes	Little Rhody	1,214	Providence
South Carolina	English king, Charles I	Palmetto State	31,055	Columbia
South Dakota	Indian tribe, Dakotas	Coyote State	77,047	Pierre
Tennessee	Ancient capital of Cherokee Indians	Volunteer State	42,244	Nashville
Texas	Indian: "Friends"	Lone Star State	267,338	Austin
Utah	Indian tribe, the Utes	Beehive State	84,916	Salt Lake City
Vermont	French: "Green mountain"	Green Mountain State	9,609	Montpelier
Virginia	Virgin Queen of England, Elizabeth I	The Old Dominion	40,817	Richmond
Washington	Our first president.	Evergreen State	68,192	Olympia
West Virginia	Virgin Queen of England, Elizabeth I	Mountain State	24,181	Charleston
Wisconsin	Indian: "Gathering of waters"	Badger State	56,154	Madison
Wyoming	Indian: "Great plains"	Equality State	97,914	Cheyenne

Population	Motto	Bird	Flower	Tree
2,404,000	"By valor and arms."	mockingbird	magnolia	magnolia
4,881,000	"The welfare of the people shall be the supreme law."	bluebird	hawthorn	flowering dogwood
785,000	"Gold and silver."	western meadowlark	bitterroot	ponderosa pine
1,568,000	"Equality before the law."	western meadowlark	goldenrod	cottonwood
660,000	"All for our country."	mountain bluebird	sagebrush	pinon
871,000	"Live free or die."	purple finch	purple lilac	white birch
7,328,000	"Liberty and prosperity."	eastern goldfinch	purple violet	red oak
1,212,000	"It grows as it goes."	road runner	yucca	pinon
17,748,000	"Ever upward."	bluebird	wild rose	sugar maple
5,577,000	"To be, rather than to seem."	cardinal	flowering dogwood	pine
652,000	"Liberty and union, now and forever; one and inseparable."	western meadowlark	wild prairie rose	American elm
10,749,000	"With God, all things are possible."	cardinal	scarlet carnation	buckeye
2,880,000	"Labor conquers all things."	scissor-tailed flycatcher	mistletoe	redbud
2,444,000	"The Union."	western meadowlark	Oregon grape	Douglas fir
11,750,000	"Virtue, liberty, and independence."	ruffed grouse	mountain laurel	hemlock
935,000	"Hope."	Rhode Island red	violet	red maple
2,918,000	"While I breathe, I hope."	Carolina wren	yellow jessamine	palmetto
690,000	"Under God the people rule."	ringnecked pheasant	pasqueflower	Black Hills spruce
4,299,000	"Agriculture and commerce."	mockingbird	iris	tulip poplar
13,014,000	"Friendship."	mockingbird	bluebonnet	pecan
1,307,000	"Industry."	seagull	sego lily	blue spruce
487,000	"Freedom and unity."	hermit thrush	red clover	sugar maple
5,148,000	"Thus always to tyrants."	cardinal	flowering dogwood	American dogwood
3,774,000	"Al-Ki." ("By and by")	willow goldfinch	western rhododendron	western hemlock
1,860,000	"Mountaineers are always free."	cardinal	great rhododendron	sugar maple
4,679,000	"Forward."	robin	wood violet	sugar maple
406,000	"Equal rights."	meadowlark	Indian paintbrush	cottonwood

Population figures from the *World Almanac*, 1980.

You can simply look at a chart, acquiring facts; or you can "read" it, acquiring not only the facts but also related ideas. Try it.

1. How many of our states were named after Indian tribes or expressions? Why? Which sounds better: the Indian word or the English translation? (Consult the column, *Origin or Meaning of Name*.)

_____

_____

_____

2. Look again at the *meanings* of the Indian words that have become state names. What do most of them have in common?

_____

_____

3. Our nicknames often tell more about us than our real names. This is true of states, too. Give the nickname for each of the following states, and describe what the nickname tells you about each state.

   a. Virginia: _____

   _____

   b. Alaska: _____

   _____

   c. Rhode Island: _____

   _____

   d. Missouri: _____

   _____

4. Four state capitals and one state were named after U.S. Presidents. List them.

   _____

   _____

5. Which bird has been "adopted" by the largest number of states? Can you suggest a logical reason why this particular bird is so popular?

   _____

   _____

6. Check the chart and find out which state "adopted" each of the following flowers. Next, turn to the map on page 172 and locate all four states. Finally, decide whether each of the flowers would thrive best in a hot or cold climate.

   a. magnolia: _____

   b. yellow jessamine: _____

   c. orange blossoms: _____

   d. pasqueflower: _____

7. The pine is, of course, common, growing in many different climates. Can you think of any other reason why the pine is so popular?

_____

_____

_____

8. What two states have the largest population? _____
What do these two states have in common? (Check the map.)

_____

_____

9. Which states have fewer than 500,000 people?

_____

_____

What, if anything, do these states have in common?

_____

_____

10. Do population and area (number of square miles) usually go together? _____
Give several specific examples to support your answer.

_____

_____

_____

11. In 1959, motorists, seeing a car with a Texas license plate, honked, held up two fingers, and grinned. The Texan usually scowled in return. Why?

_____

_____

_____

12. Name a state whose motto suggests faith in each of the following. (Do not name any state more than once.)

unity _____   freedom _____

democracy _____   equality _____

God _____   progress _____

13. Consider carefully the bird, flower, tree, and motto of Oklahoma. Do these tell you anything about the legislature or people of that state?

_____

_____

_____

_____

READING A FLAG

Each of the fifty states has its own flag. On the facing page you can see these flags, unfortunately not in full color and not large enough to see some of the fine details. But you can see most of the designs. Again, look—relate to information on the map (172) or chart (174–177)—think. Then answer these questions.

1. Some of the state flags are clearly related to information given in the chart. Show how this is true about the following state flags.

   Washington: _____

   _____

   South Carolina: _____

   _____

   Louisiana: _____

   _____

   Arizona: _____

   _____

2. Colorado's state colors are blue and white. On the flag, the top and bottom thirds are blue and the middle third is white. Why is the "C" red?

   _____

   _____

3. How does Georgia's flag show her pride in being one of the thirteen original states?

   _____

   _____

4. Florida's flag shows an Indian girl scattering flowers. Why?

   _____

   _____

5. If you know anything about astronomy, you know that the stars on Alaska's flag represent the Big Dipper and the North Star. Make a reasonable guess as to why Alaska chose this particular design for her flag.

   _____

   _____

6. Why is it appropriate that on her flag, Virginia should have a female warrior rather than a male warrior standing triumphant over the figure of tyranny?

   _____

   _____

7. On its flag, Michigan has an elk and a moose supporting a shield. Which other animal would be more appropriate? Why?

   _____

   _____

Alabama Alaska Arizona Arkansas California

Colorado Connecticut Delaware Florida Georgia

Hawaii Idaho Illinois Indiana Iowa

Kansas Kentucky Louisiana Maine Maryland

Massachusetts Michigan Minnesota Mississippi Missouri

Montana Nebraska Nevada New Hampshire New Jersey

New Mexico New York North Carolina North Dakota Ohio

Oklahoma Oregon Pennsylvania Rhode Island South Carolina

South Dakota Tennessee Texas Utah Vermont

Virginia Washington West Virginia Wisconsin Wyoming

CURIOUS ABOUT THE FABULOUS FIFTY?

Of course, you're curious! As you may have realized by now, the more you know about something, the more you want to know. Answer the questions below and you will add many curious facts to your collection. Use any library reference . . . you know how to!

1. A state named "Frankland" actually existed, although it was never officially recognized. What is the true story about Frankland: how it came into being, how long it lasted, how it ceased to exist? (Look under Tennessee.)

_____

_____

_____

_____

2. Why does Nevada have on its flag the words, "Battle Born"?

_____

_____

3. Texas is known as the "Lone Star State" and has a "lone star" on its flag. Why?

_____

_____

4. About how much per mile did we pay when we bought Alaska from the Russians in 1867?

_____

_____

5. How come *nobody* knows whether North Dakota or South Dakota was first admitted to the Union?

_____

_____

6. Talking about North Dakota—it's famous for its Bad Lands. One envisions outlaws running around with six-shooters; but, of course, this isn't true. What *are* the "Bad Lands"? How did they come into existence? What do they look like?

_____

_____

_____

_____

7. One of the oddest nicknames is the "Tar Heel State"—for beautiful North Carolina. Why do you suppose North Carolina picked up this strange and not very pleasant nickname?

_____

_____

8. Every year on October 19, the citizens of Maryland celebrate "Peggy Stewart Day." One hint: it all started in 1775. Who was PEGGY STEWART, and what happened on October 19, 1775, that everyone likes to remember?

_____

_____

_____

_____

9. In North Carolina in the 16th century, a colony was established that became known as The Lost Colony. Find out everything you can about The Lost Colony and write it below.

_____

_____

_____

_____

10. As you already know, Connecticut is sometimes called "The Nutmeg State." Find out *why* Connecticut is called "The Nutmeg State," and then explain why the nickname is both complimentary and uncomplimentary.

_____

_____

_____

11. San Juan Island lies between the state of Washington and Vancouver Island. San Juan was settled by both British and American pioneers. Around 1855 a barnyard dispute caused a great many arguments, and the whole thing wasn't settled until 1872. Describe the "barnyard dispute" and the result of arbitration. (Did the pigs win, or the potato patch, or maybe the sheep?)

_____

_____

_____

_____

12. Scattered throughout our fifty states are quite a few "curiosities." Describe each of the following "curiosities" briefly.

Ice Mountain (West Virginia): _____

_____

Old Faithful (Wyoming): _____

_____

Mauna Loa (Hawaii): _____

_____

TIME OUT FOR WORD GAMES USING THE FABULOUS FIFTY!

I. You can find just about anything in the state names. For example, you can find FOAL in FLOridA, by dropping the "r," "i," and "d," and rearranging the remaining four letters. Or you can find a LION in ILliNOis. Can you find the following?

a. A noun that is part of a lion's attire in MAINE __ __ __ __

b. A noun that is an article of clothing in UTAH __ __ __

c. A noun that names something that indicates wind direction in NEVADA __ __ __ __ __

d. A verb meaning "to cut' in WYOMING __ __ __

e. A verb meaning to go from one place to another in VERMONT __ __ __ __

f. A verb meaning to make a musical sound in MASSACHUSETTS __ __ __

g. An adjective meaning light brown in MINNESOTA __ __ __

h. An adjective meaning tart, not sweet, in MISSOURI __ __ __ __

i. An adjective meaning ashy, colorless in PENNSYLVANIA __ __ __ __

j. An adverb meaning unreasonably, wildly in MARYLAND __ __ __ __ __

k. An adverb meaning reasonably, logically in PENNSYLVANIA __ __ __ __ __ __

l. A pronoun—third person, feminine—in MASSACHUSETTS __ __ __

m. A pronoun—third person, masculine—in NEW HAMPSHIRE __ __

n. A pronoun—third person, neuter—in CONNECTICUT __ __

o. A conjunction in INDIANA __ __ __

p. Another conjunction in NORTH CAROLINA __ __ __

q. Still another conjunction in OREGON __ __

r. A preposition in CALIFORNIA __ __ __

s. A different preposition in MONTANA __ __

t. A still different preposition in FLORIDA __ __

II. If we could form fifty states into one United States, *you* should be able to form fifty words from the two words, UNITED STATES. Condition: no word of fewer than three letters. (If you're *really* good, you should be able to form 100 words!)

_____ _____ _____ _____ _____

_____ _____ _____ _____ _____

_____ _____ _____ _____ _____

_____ _____ _____ _____ _____

_____ _____ _____ _____ _____

_____ _____ _____ _____ _____

_____ _____ _____ _____ _____

_____ _____ _____ _____ _____

III. Just as you can find words in state names, so you can find state names in other word combinations. But this is tricky! In each of the following sentences, the name of a state is hidden. Your job is to find the state. The first sentence is decoded to act as a guide. Below are the names of the eight states that appear in the sentences.

Alabama	Georgia	Utah
Alaska	Indiana	Vermont
Delaware	Oregon	

1. A dog can run fast, *but a h*are can run faster.   **Utah** _____

2. She bought the large or giant-size package of detergent. _____

3. Nothing that happens in a lab amazes me any longer. _____

4. In Venice, more gondolas are needed than in New York. _____

5. In my mind, I analyze an idea before I write about it. _____

6. My check, enclosed, will cover months May, June, and July. _____

7. No one is more comical a skater than Jabez, the clown. _____

8. People who cannot abide law are apt to become outlaws. _____

IV. Finally, here is one more word game using state names. Just find the parts and you will identify the state. The first one, already completed, will show you the way.

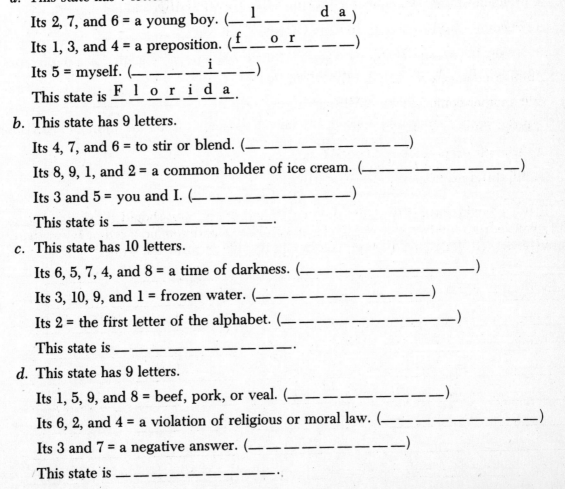

a. This state has 7 letters.

Its 2, 7, and 6 = a young boy. (_ l _ _ _ d a)

Its 1, 3, and 4 = a preposition. (f _ o r _ _ _)

Its 5 = myself. (_ _ _ _ i _ _)

This state is F l o r i d a.

b. This state has 9 letters.

Its 4, 7, and 6 = to stir or blend. (_ _ _ _ _ _ _ _ _)

Its 8, 9, 1, and 2 = a common holder of ice cream. (_ _ _ _ _ _ _ _ _)

Its 3 and 5 = you and I. (_ _ _ _ _ _ _ _ _)

This state is _ _ _ _ _ _ _ _ _.

c. This state has 10 letters.

Its 6, 5, 7, 4, and 8 = a time of darkness. (_ _ _ _ _ _ _ _ _ _)

Its 3, 10, 9, and 1 = frozen water. (_ _ _ _ _ _ _ _ _ _)

Its 2 = the first letter of the alphabet. (_ _ _ _ _ _ _ _ _ _)

This state is _ _ _ _ _ _ _ _ _ _.

d. This state has 9 letters.

Its 1, 5, 9, and 8 = beef, pork, or veal. (_ _ _ _ _ _ _ _ _)

Its 6, 2, and 4 = a violation of religious or moral law. (_ _ _ _ _ _ _ _ _)

Its 3 and 7 = a negative answer. (_ _ _ _ _ _ _ _ _)

This state is _ _ _ _ _ _ _ _ _.

ANGLING A PARAGRAPH

As you know by now, *angling* is important to good writing. If you simply write about the trees of the fifty states, you will have a dull paragraph. But if you *angle* it properly, you may well have a fascinating one!

I. *State Trees.*   You can find plenty of angles just by studying the chart.

a. Many states favor the evergreen, but only one favors the pecan.

b. Many state trees reflect the economy of a region. (For example, the sugar maple in Vermont reflects the importance of the manufacture of maple sugar and maple syrup.)

c. A few state trees are unusual and should be related in a special way to the states that adopted them. (For example, Arizona, with much desert land, chose the "palo-verde"—a spiny, almost leafless shrub that grows well in a hot climate and that has showy, yellow flowers, like the sun.)

You add a fourth possible angle. THINK!

d. _____

_____

_____

II. *State Birds.*   Suggest one possible angle for a paragraph about state birds.

_____

III. *State Flowers.*   Suggest one possible angle for a paragraph about state flowers.

_____

IV. *Origin or Meaning of State Names.*   Suggest one possible angle for a paragraph about the origin or meaning of state names.

_____

V. Now—write a paragraph, using any one of the angles listed in I through IV. Keep your angle firmly in mind while you are writing the paragraph.

_____

_____

_____

_____

_____

_____

_____

_____

_____

_____

_____

VI. On pages 178 and 179 there are angles for at least a dozen different and interesting paragraphs. Reread these pages and select one angle that interests you.

_____

Write a paragraph using this angle—and keeping the angle firmly in mind.

_____
_____
_____
_____
_____

VII. On pages 182 and 183 there are angles for at least twelve fascinating paragraphs. Reread these pages and select one angle that interests you. Then write a paragraph, using this angle. Keep the angle firmly in mind while you are writing.

_____
_____
_____
_____
_____
_____

VIII. On pages 172 and 173, and on pages 180 and 181, are angles for at least eighteen good paragraphs. Reread these pages; select an angle that interests you; write.

_____
_____
_____
_____
_____

IX. From any one of the preceding pages on "States," select material that will make an amusing anecdote (see page 24). You will find the material on page 183 especially good. Write the anecdote, keeping it light, and using some dialogue.

_____
_____
_____
_____
_____

THE GRAND FINALE!

Now for the Grand Finale of the Grand Finale!

You have been thinking about the fabulous fifty states. You have manipulated them, explored them, researched them, thought about them, and written about them. You probably know more about them now than do most people living in this country. So you are truly a mini-expert!

Think about them again. Select an angle for a full-length essay. Choose an angle that really interests you.

You may wish to write about your own state and how it compares to other states. You may wish to write about a particular group of states: the Southern states, for example. Or you may wish to write about all the states.

You may wish to write about state populations—or state mottoes—or state nicknames. You may wish to write about admission dates—or geographical boundaries.

The choice is yours. Choose any angle. Then . . .

    . . . Take notes.

    . . . Think.

    . . . Make a rough outline.

    . . . Think.

    . . . Write a first draft on scrap paper.

    . . . Think.

    . . . Revise.

    . . . Copy your completed polished essay on this page and the next.

Go!

THE GRAND FINALE! (Continued)

_____

_____

_____

_____

_____

_____

_____

_____

_____

_____

_____

_____

_____

_____

_____

_____

_____

_____

_____

_____

_____

_____

_____

_____

Now—isn't that a fine essay? It should be! Compare it to some of the writing you did in the first section of this book, and you should feel really proud of the improvement you have made. In the future, remember: be CURIOUS—satisfy your CURIOSITY—and you will always have something to talk about and write about!

PLANTS WITH UNUSUAL NAMES
(See Question III on page 169.)

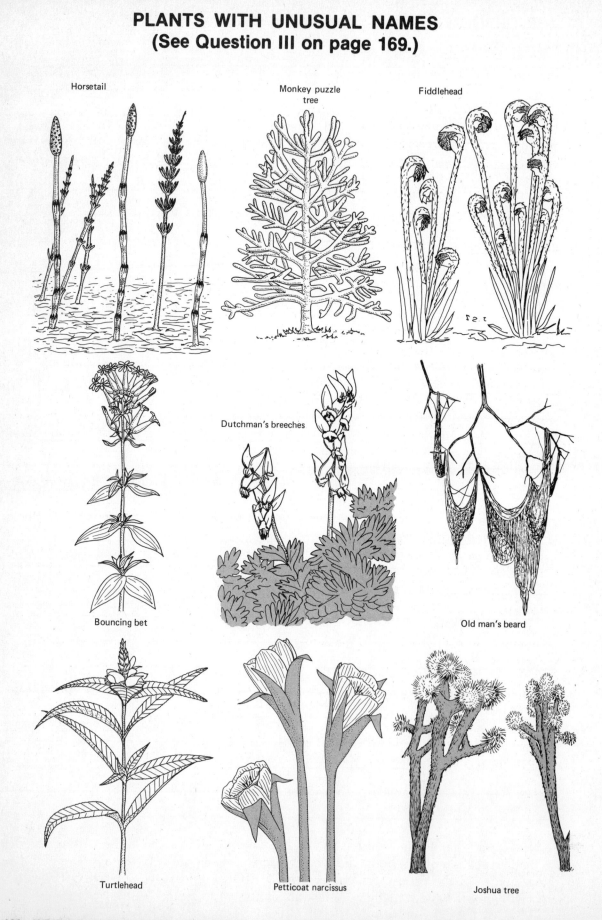

Horsetail

Monkey puzzle tree

Fiddlehead

Dutchman's breeches

Bouncing bet

Old man's beard

Turtlehead

Petticoat narcissus

Joshua tree

GLOSSARY

alliteration: the deliberate use of several words beginning with the same sound, 52, 55, 67, 82, 94, 112, 124 (Examples: *t*all and *t*owering *t*rees; *n*ice, *n*ewsy, and *n*atural)

anagram: a word made by rearranging the letters of another word, 104, 144 (Examples: SKATE rearranged becomes STAKE or STEAK.)

anecdote: a very short story, interesting and possibly humorous, about some event, 24, 158, 187

antonyms: words that have opposite meanings, 2, 35, 150 (Examples: *fine* and *coarse; long* and *short*)

atlas: a book of maps, 140

autobiography: a story of a person's life written by oneself, 16, 18, 72–74

bibliography: a list of books, magazine articles, and newspaper articles about a particular subject, 163

biography: a story of a person's life written by another person, 18

catechism: any book containing questions and answers, 22

clause: a group of words having a subject and a verb (See **main clause** and **subordinate clause**.)

complex sentence: a sentence consisting of two simple sentences connected in such a way that one is dependent on the other. The dependent (or subordinate) clause is introduced by a **subordinate conjunction:** *if, when, because, while,* etc., 84, 101, 117, 118, 120, 130, 135 (Example: *Consumers will have more money to spend* if *taxes are cut.*)

compound: describes something with two or more parts, 78

compound object: a simple sentence containing two or more objects, 78 (Example: Pigs can be taught to carry *schoolbooks* and *newspapers.*)

compound sentence: a sentence containing two or more simple sentences, with separate but related ideas. The parts are usually connected by the **coordinate conjunction** *and, but,* or *or,* 78, 101 (Example: *Pigs are good fighters,* and *they can bite savagely.*)

compound subject: a simple sentence whose subject contains two or more parts, 78 (Example: *Insects* and *earthworms* are often eaten by pigs.)

compound verb: a simple sentence containing two or more verbs, 78 (Example: Pigs can *climb* ladders and *balance* balls on their snouts.)

concrete poetry: a kind of poetry in which the words actually form an image or picture, 106

conjunction: a connecting word used to combine simple sentences. (See **complex sentence** and **compound sentence**.)

consonants: See vowels.

couplet: two lines that rhyme, 4, 10, 140, 169

declarative sentence: a sentence that makes a statement, 4, 10, 16, 21, 22, 57, 83 (Example: Blondes have more fun.)

dialogue: a conversation between two or more people; also, the words spoken by the characters of a story or play, 22, 40, 71, 112, 134

documentary: a presentation of facts about someone, something, or some event, 148

exclamatory sentence: a sentence that expresses strong feeling, 16, 22, 57, 83 (Example: Those jeans—they're gorgeous!)

fable: a very short story that teaches a lesson, 6

generalization: a sentence that states an idea briefly, 12, 28, 33, 58, 59

homophones: two or more words that sound alike, but have different meanings and different spellings, 20, 100, 169 (Examples: *tail* and *tale; sight* and *site*)

idiom: an expression with a special meaning not clear from the usual meaning of the words in the expression, 171 (Example: "being on pins and needles" means "to be in a state of anxiety.")

imperative sentence: a sentence that gives an order, a command, 16, 22, 57, 83 (Example: Put those jeans in the wash today.)

interrogative sentence: a sentence that asks a question, 4, 10, 16, 21, 22, 57, 83, 151 (Example: Do blondes have more fun?)

limerick: a humorous five-line poem. The first, second, and fifth lines are fairly long, and they rhyme. The third and fourth lines are shorter, and they rhyme, 154

main clause: a group of words that contains a subject and a verb and stands alone to express a complete thought, 135 (Example: *Unemployment will decline* when our factories return to full production.)

onomatopoeia: the use of a word whose sound imitates its meaning, 55, 82 (Examples: *hum, buzz, crash, hiss*)

palindrome: a word that is spelled the same forward and backward, 110 (Examples: *eve* and *radar*)

parallel sentences: sentences that match each other. They go in the same direction, and their parts are related in a similar way, 38, 132, 140, 166

paraphrase: a restatement in different words, 95, 146

parody: a comic imitation of a literary work that makes fun of the original, 118

period: end punctuation of a declarative sentence, 4

phrase: a group of words that lacks both a subject and a verb (See **preposition.**)

plot: the action that takes place in a story, 142

prefix: a syllable added to the beginning of another word, 10, 14, 33, 89, 103 (Examples: TELE in *telephone*, AUTO in *automobile*, SUB in *submarine*)

preposition: a word that shows relationship. Combined with a noun, a preposition forms a prepositional phrase, 130, 137 (Example: *Under the tin can* is a pink satin tablecloth.)

prepositional phrase: See **preposition.**

pun: a play on words, 55, 83

quatrain: a four-line poem, 46

question mark: end punctuation of an interrogative sentence, 4

revision: a corrected or improved version; also, the act of correcting or improving written material, 44, 152, 154, 158, 160

simile: a comparison using "like" or "as," 112 (Example: Her teeth are like pearls.)

simple sentence: contains one subject, one verb, and expresses one idea, 78, 101 (Example: The hope of all the world is peace.)

slang: the nonstandard use of a word, 49, 71 (Examples: a *pay-off*, a *well-heeled* person)

subordinate clause: a group of words that contains a subject and a verb, but cannot stand alone to express a complete thought, 117, 118, 120, 135 (Examples: if it doesn't rain; because I was late; while the band played)

synonym: a word that has the same meaning as another word or words, 106, 137, 164 (Examples: *glide* and *skate, story* and *tale*)

thesaurus: a dictionary of synonyms and antonyms, that is, of words with similar meanings and words with opposite meanings, 106, 137, 164

transitional words: words like *next, then, etc.*, that link one sentence to another, 140

vowels: the letters *a, e, i, o, u.* All the other letters of the alphabet are the **consonants,** 36, 42, 54, 69, 137

INDEX

action verbs: 164, 166

adjectives: 37, 94

alliteration: (glossary), 52, 55, 67, 82, 94, 112, 124

anagram: (glossary), 104, 144

anecdote: (glossary), 24, 158, 187

angle: 160, 186, 187, 188

antonyms: (glossary), 2, 35, 150

atlas: (glossary), 140

autobiography: (glossary), 16, 18, 72–74

bibliography: (glossary), 163

biography: (glossary), 18

bread-and-butter letter: 146

business letter: 114

catechism: (glossary), 22

clause:
  main: (glossary), 135
  subordinate: (glossary), 117, 118, 120, 135

combining sentences: 152, 164

comma (to set off an introductory subordinate clause): 117

complex sentence: (glossary), 84, 101, 117, 118, 120, 130, 135

compound:
  object: (glossary), 78
  sentence: (glossary), 78, 101
  subject: (glossary), 78
  verb: (glossary), 78
  words: 69

concrete poetry: (glossary), 106

conjunction:
  coordinate: (glossary, compound sentence), 78, 101
  subordinate: (glossary, complex sentence), 84, 101, 117, 118, 120, 130, 135

consonants: (glossary, vowels), 36, 42, 137

coordinate conjunction: (glossary, compound sentence), 78, 101

couplet: (glossary), 4, 10, 140, 169

declarative sentence: (glossary), 4, 10, 16, 21, 22, 57, 83

dialogue: 22, 40, 71, 112, 134

documentary: (glossary), 148

exclamatory sentence: (glossary), 16, 22, 57, 83

fable: (glossary), 6

generalization: (glossary), 12, 28, 33, 58, 59

graphic thinking: 44, 67

homophones: (glossary), 20, 100, 169

idiom: (glossary), 171

imperative sentence: (glossary), 16, 22, 57, 83

interrogative sentence: (glossary), 4, 10, 16, 21, 22, 57, 83, 151

invitation, writing an: 108

letters:
  bread-and-butter: 146
  business: 114
  of invitation: 108

limerick: (glossary), 154

lists, making: 26–30, 60–65

main clause: (glossary), 135

object, compound: (glossary), 78

onomatopoeia: (glossary), 55, 82

outlining: 16, 18, 58, 72, 78, 142, 148, 160

palindrome: (glossary), 110

parallel sentences: (glossary), 38, 132, 140, 166

paraphrase: (glossary), 95, 146

parody: (glossary), 118

period: (glossary), 4

phrase: (glossary, preposition), 130, 137

plot: (glossary), 142

poll, taking a: 12, 37, 123, 156

prefix: (glossary), 10, 14, 33, 89, 103

preposition: (glossary), 130, 137

prepositional phrase: (glossary, preposition), 130, 137

psychological thinking: 44

pun: (glossary), 55, 83

quatrain: (glossary), 46

question mark: (glossary), 4

questions and answers, writing of: 10,
   22, 63, 111, 151

reference books:
   almanac practice: 9
   atlas: 140
   Bartlett's *Familiar Quotations*: 77
   Brewer's *A Dictionary of Phrase
      and Fable*: 3, 77
   card catalog: 163
   dictionary practice: 3, 15, 43, 48–
      52, 69, 77, 94, 129, 137, 138, 163
   encyclopedia practice: 35, 43, 105,
      129, 145, 163
   Guinness Book of World Records:
      3, 9, 21, 43, 77, 105
   Kane's *Famous First Facts and Rec-
      ords*: 9, 43, 105
   The People's Almanac, Wallechin-
      sky and Wallace: 43
   *Readers' Guide to Periodical Lit-
      erature*: 105, 163
   Roget's *Thesaurus of English Words
      and Phrases*; 106, 137, 164
repetition: 24, 40, 132
revision: (glossary), 44, 152, 154,
   158, 160

sentences: (See writing sentences)
simile: (glossary), 112
simple sentence: (glossary), 78, 101
slang: (glossary), 49, 71
styling sentences: 4, 10, 44, 72, 78, 83,
   84, 100, 130, 151, 152, 164
subordinate:
   clause: (glossary), 117, 118, 120, 135
   conjunction: (glossary, **complex
      sentence**), 84, 117, 118, 120, 135
synonym: (glossary), 106, 137, 164

thesaurus: (glossary), 106, 137, 164
topic sentences: 24, 166
transitional words: (glossary), 140

verbs:
   action: 164, 166
   compound: (glossary), 78

vocabulary (*related to chapters*):
   3, 4 (*hair*); 9 (*telephone*);
   15 (*denim*); 21, 22 (*dog*);
   37 (*cookie*); 55 (*comic strip*);
   77 (*pig*); 89 (*shopping center*);
   95 (*weather*); 105 (*skating*);
   111 (*robot*); 123 (*fast-food*);
   129 (*tin-can*); 138, 139 (*boat*);
   145 (*bread*); 157 (*peeve*)
vowels: (glossary), 36, 42, 54, 69, 137

words and phrases:
   manipulation (games, puzzles, rid-
      dles): 8, 34, 35, 68, 69, 70, 76, 88,
      100, 101, 102, 103, 104, 122, 135,
      136, 144, 162, 170, 171, 184, 185

   See also **action verbs, adjectives,
   antonyms, compound words,
   homophones, onomatopoeia, prefixes, slang, synonyms, transitional words, vocabulary.**

writing:
sentences:
   complex: (glossary), 84, 101, 117,
      120, 130, 135
   compound: (glossary), 78, 101
   declarative: (glossary), 4, 10, 16,
      21, 22, 57, 83
   defining: 10, 14, 33, 48, 49, 69, 138,
      163
   exclamatory: (glossary), 16, 22, 57,
      83
   imperative: (glossary), 16, 22, 57, 83
   interrogative: (glossary), 4, 10, 16,
      21, 22, 57, 83, 151
   parallel: (glossary), 38, 132, 140, 166
   simple: (glossary), 78, 101
   styling: 4, 10, 44, 72, 78, 83, 84,
      100, 130, 151, 152, 164
   topic: 24, 166

paragraphs:
   anecdote: 24, 154, 158, 187
   description: 6, 18, 32, 96, 112, 124,
      166, 169
   directions: 38
   general: 24, 30, 120, 166, 186
   generalization to details: 12, 18, 24,
      26, 28, 46, 52, 92, 132, 187
   persuasion: 38